The Quotable American

The Quotable American

Edited by
Alex Barnett

THE LYONS PRESS
Guilford, Connecticut
An imprint of The Globe Pequot Press

10 9 8 7 6 5 4 3 2 1

Printed in the United States of America

Library of Congress Cataloging-in-Publication Data is available on file.

ISBN 1-58574-568-5

Acknowledgments

Many thanks to Tom McCarthy, Vivian Barnett, and Eileen Kane.

Contents

Introduction

The story of America is nothing short of astonishing. It is the story of a people of remarkable diversity, some seeking advancement, others fleeing oppression, who settled together on the edge of a vast wilderness with little in common other than a determination to shape their own lives. Within decades, they would join together to defeat Britain in a war of independence and create the world's first modern democracy. From there thirteen small colonies grew with breathtaking speed to become the wealthiest, most powerful, most inventive nation the world had ever seen.

The aim of this collection is to explore the many facets of our national character through the words of Americans: the courage of Washington, the tenacity of John Paul Jones, the irreverence of Twain, the humanity of Lincoln, the optimism of Franklin D. Roosevelt, the solitary defiance of Rosa Parks, and the revolutionary idealism of Thomas Jefferson, Susan B. Anthony, and Martin Luther King.

What is it about America that has produced a national character so influential, so distinctive, and so quotable? The list of factors is endless, but three unique aspects of our history stand out: our democratic tradition, our landscape, and the diversity of our people.

> Were it left to me to decide whether we should
> have a government without newspapers, or news-

papers without a government, I should not hesitate a moment to prefer the latter.

THOMAS JEFFERSON, 1787

When the first settlers reached North America in the early 1600s, democracy as we think of it now did not exist. The early colonists brought with them the political structures of England: they established legislatures modeled on the British parliament, which were overseen by a governor, often an aristocrat appointed by the king as his representative. But as these institutions were transplanted to the rugged, egalitarian environment of the New World, they soon began to change.

Many of the first Americans, such as the Pilgrims and Puritans of Massachusetts, were Protestant dissenters who had broken with the Church of England and looked to the New World as a refuge from persecution. They brought with them a tradition of independence, as well as the quintessentially democratic institution of the "town meeting." They were soon joined by farmers, laborers, and artisans, along with a smattering of aristocrats, debtors, and crooks—people drawn mostly from the lower classes of Europe who had more to gain than to lose in a risky adventure. Not surprisingly, the legislatures they created looked different. In England, the upper house of parliament was determined by heredity; the lower house was technically elected, but voting rights depended on property ownership and religious affiliation, so in practice very few people could vote. In America too, only male property owners could vote, but because of the abundance of cheap land, few were excluded for that reason. The growing diversity of religious faiths in the colonies made it difficult to tie voting rights to church membership. The upshot was that far more people voted in the colonies than in England. And in the absence of the well-defined class system of Britain, Americans were less inclined to elect their social superiors and more likely to demand meaningful representation. As time went by, emboldened by their distance from England, the legislators began to take power away from the governors.

By most accounts, the Revolution was precipitated by trade and taxes. At the end of the French and Indian Wars in 1763, England made a renewed effort to raise money from the colonies and control their trading with other nations; no longer threatened by the French in North America, the colonists began to resist. But underneath the particulars of the tax laws were the startling facts that the colonists had grown fundamentally apart from England, they had begun to view themselves as nothing less than a new people, and they now saw their independence as a right, not a privilege.

With the Declaration of Independence and the Constitution in 1789, the colonists articulated a political philosophy and invented a new form of government that have gained acceptance throughout the world in the two centuries since. The authors of the Declaration borrowed ideas already circulating in Europe, but they stated them with unprecedented boldness and clarity: All men are created equal and endowed with natural rights, including life, liberty, and the pursuit of happiness; governments exist to secure these rights; and legitimate governments derive their authority from the consent of the governed. With its shrewd distribution of powers, its firm separation of church and state, and its vigorous protection of individual liberties, the American Constitution is one of the most influential political documents in history. And underlying both is the characteristically American faith that the judgment of a free people is more trustworthy than the dictates of an elite.

> Go West, young man, and grow up with the country.
>
> HORACE GREELEY, NEWSPAPER EDITOR, 1850

As the Revolution ended, the conquest of the continent was just beginning. The first settlers landed on the edge of a forest wilderness that resembled nothing in Europe, with its tidy farms and ancient cities. In the late 1700s, settlement was still confined to a narrow band along the eastern coast, and "the West" meant the Appalachian Mountains. That began to change in 1803, when the United States paid $15 million to acquire from France the Louisiana territory extending from the Mississippi River to the Rocky Mountains, and from the Gulf of Mexico to Canada—in one stroke doubling the area of the country. The Great Plains of the interior were a vast, flat grassland of amazing size and emptiness that travelers likened to a desert, or an ocean. The western plains were too arid for anything but grazing, but the eastern portions offered the topsoil and rainfall necessary to grow huge quantities of wheat, corn, and oats.

In the mid-1800s, fired by the idea of Manifest Destiny, America expanded rapidly across the continent through a combination of diplomacy, bargaining, and war. By 1850 our borders reached almost to their modern shape, encompassing the dramatic Western mountain ranges, the near-desert of the southwestern Great Basin, the Mediterranean climate of southern California, and the rainy forests of the Pacific Northwest. The lure of the West and the process of its settlement had a profound effect on the country. The frontier was wild, empty, dangerous, and full of possibility. Like their ancestors who left Europe, the pioneers were tough, ambitious, self-reliant, and optimistic, always ready to pull up stakes and make a fresh start somewhere else. By 1850 almost half of the population lived west of the Appalachians. In 1893, as the frontier line reached the Pacific and disappeared, the historian Frederick Turner paused to describe in a now-famous essay the American character that was born on the push West:

> To the frontier the American intellect owes its
> striking characteristics. That coarseness and
> strength combined with acuteness and inquisitive-
> ness; that practical, inventive turn of mind . . . that

restless, nervous energy; that dominant individualism, working for good and for evil, and withal
that buoyancy and exuberance which comes with
freedom.

THE SIGNIFICANCE OF THE FRONTIER IN AMERICAN
HISTORY

In 1867 sub-arctic Alaska was purchased from Russia and in 1898 tropical Hawaii was annexed, bringing America to its modern dimensions.

His foreparents came to America in immigrant
ships. My foreparents came to America in slave
ships. But whatever the original ships, we are both
in the same boat tonight.

JESSE JACKSON, 1988

From the beginning, the colonists were a diverse group. Before the Revolution, the European population was primarily English, Irish, Scottish, German, and Dutch. By 1760, about one fifth of the population of the colonies was of African descent, most of them slaves who had been brought to the southern colonies to farm rice, tobacco, indigo, and later cotton.

Between the Revolutionary War and 1815, Europeans arrived in the New World at a trickle, but by the mid-1800s immigration surged due to economic hardship in Europe, the potato blight in Ireland, and a growing awareness of the political freedom and economic opportunity in America. An estimated 1.7 million Europeans arrived in the 1840s, and 2.3 million in the 1850s. Most of the new arrivals were from Britain, Ireland, and Germany, but Swiss, French, Poles, Russians, and Italians now entered the mix in significant numbers. This influx was a major factor in the extraordinary economic growth of the country before the Civil War. In 1815, America was a sleepy agrarian nation of 8.5 million; by 1860 it was a rising industrial power of 30 million, comparable in population and output to England, Germany, and France.

Immigration accelerated after the Civil War. Between 1900 and 1920, an additional 14 million arrived, but now most immigrants no longer came from Northern Europe. The new Americans were Russians and Poles, Italians and Greeks, Czechs and Serbo-Croatians. Since the 1960s, the majority of new immigrants have come from Asia and Latin America. To this astonishing diversity America owes its great cities, its economic and intellectual wealth, its music and movies, its literature and cuisine, its tradition of openness and tolerance, and its perennial capacity for change and reinvention.

When Thomas Jefferson composed the promise that all men are created equal, the war was just beginning and the Declaration was nothing but a dream. The Declaration was still a dream in 1830 when Andrew Jackson signed the Indian Removal Act, and in 1865 when slavery was abolished, and in 1920 when women finally won the right to vote. But the dream it inspired has created America and reshaped the world. No nation in history has attracted such a diversity of people to its shores, and no nation has done more to protect the freedom of its citizens—to worship, to speak, to dissent. Together, the diversity and freedom of America promise that the flaws of our country will continue to be exposed, and we will approximate more and more closely the republic that the founders described.

The attacks of September 11, 2001, have permanently altered the skyline of New York City and they will surely change our country. We have lost a sense of safety, invulnerability, and detachment. We have embarked upon a new kind of war with an uncertain end. It is likely that we will sacrifice a degree of privacy and mobility in the name of security. And yet, in our grief and outrage, we are reminded of our connections to one another, and of the values that we cherish as Americans—of the courage of the rescue workers who died trying to saving others, the compassion of the thousands who waited to give blood, and the independence and resilience of ordinary Americans everywhere who in little acts of defiance refused to let fear direct their lives. Our country has met terrible adversity in its past and survived. If our history is any guide, we will meet the tragedy of September 11 with determination, strength, and humanity, and emerge a better and stronger nation.

Defining Moments

Hang a lantern aloft in the belfry arch
Of the North Church tower as a signal light,—
One, if by land, and two, if by sea;
And I on the opposite shore will be,
Ready to ride and spread the alarm
Through every Middlesex village and farm.

HENRY WADSWORTH LONGFELLOW
"PAUL REVERE'S RIDE" IN *TALES OF A WAYSIDE INN* (1863–1874)

What a glorious morning is this!

SAMUEL ADAMS, AMERICAN REVOLUTIONARY LEADER, UPON
HEARING GUNSHOTS AT LEXINGTON, APRIL 19, 1775

The time is now near at hand which must probably determine whether Americans are to be freemen or slaves; whether they are to have any property they can call their own. The fate of unborn millions will now depend, under God, on the courage and conduct of this army. We have, therefore, to resolve to conquer or die.

GEORGE WASHINGTON, GENERAL ORDERS, 2 JULY 1776

We must indeed all hang together, or, most assuredly, we shall all hang separately.

BENJAMIN FRANKLIN, ON SIGNING THE DECLARATION OF
INDEPENDENCE, JULY 4, 1776

We have lived long, but this is the noblest work of our lives.

ROBERT R. LIVINGSTON, AT THE SIGNING OF THE LOUISIANA
PURCHASE, MAY 1803

Remember the Alamo!

SIDNEY SHERMAN, AT THE BATTLE OF SAN JACINTO, APRIL 21, 1836

———•═•———

By the Eternal, they shall not sleep on our soil!

GENERAL ANDREW JACKSON, UPON LEARNING THAT A BRITISH ARMY
HAD LANDED NEAR NEW ORLEANS, DECEMBER 23, 1814

The tract you have ceded will soon be surveyed and sold, and immediately afterwards will be occupied by a white population. You will soon be in a state of starvation. You will commit depredations upon the property of our citizens. You will be resisted, punished, perhaps killed. Now, is it not better peaceably to remove to a fine, fertile country, occupied by your own kindred, and where you can raise all the necessaries of life, and where game is yet abundant?

ANDREW JACKSON, U.S. PRESIDENT, ADDRESSING THE CHIEFS OF THE SEMINOLES, FEBRUARY 16, 1835

I, John Brown, am now quite certain that the crimes of this guilty land will never be purged away but with blood.

JOHN BROWN, WRITTEN ON THE DAY OF HIS EXECUTION, DECEMBER 2, 1859

There is Jackson with his Virginians, standing like a stone wall. Let us determine to die here, and we will conquer!

BARNARD ELLIOT BEE, A CONFEDERATE OFFICER, AT THE BATTLE OF BULL RUN, JULY 21, 1861

Fourscore and seven years ago our fathers brought forth upon this continent a new nation, conceived in liberty, and dedicated to the proposition that all men are created equal. Now we are engaged in a great civil war, testing whether that nation, or any nation so conceived and so dedicated, can long endure.

ABRAHAM LINCOLN, GETTYSBURG ADDRESS, NOVEMBER 19, 1863

APRIL 7, 1865

LIEUT. GEN. U.S. GRANT:

GENERAL: I have received your note of this date. Though not entertaining the opinion you express on the hopelessness of further resistance on the part of the Army of Northern Virginia, I reciprocate your desire to avoid useless effusion of blood, and therefore ask the terms you will offer on condition of its surrender.

R. E. LEE, GENERAL.

ROBERT E. LEE SURRENDERED TO ULYSSES S. GRANT AT APPOMATTOX COURTHOUSE TWO DAYS LATER.

Now he belongs to the ages.

EDWIN M. STANTON, SECRETARY OF WAR, AT LINCOLN'S BEDSIDE
WHEN THE PRESIDENT DIED ON APRIL 15, 1865

May God continue the unity of our Country as this
Railroad unites the two great Oceans of the world

INSCRIPTION ON THE GOLDEN SPIKE THAT JOINED THE CENTRAL AND
UNION PACIFIC RAILROADS AT PROMONTORY SUMMIT, UTAH, ON
MAY 10, 1869

Mr. Watson, come here, I want you.

ALEXANDER GRAHAM BELL, TO HIS ASSISTANT IN HISTORY'S FIRST
TELEPHONE CONVERSATION, MARCH 10, 1876

Up to and including 1880, the country had a frontier of settlement but at present the unsettled area has been so broken into by isolated bodies of settlement that there can hardly be said to be a frontier line.

BULLETIN OF THE SUPERINTENDENT OF THE CENSUS FOR 1890

Success four flights Thursday morning all against twenty one mile wind started from Level with engine power alone speed through air thirty one miles longest 57 second inform Press home Christmas.

ORVILLE WRIGHT, TELEGRAM TO HIS FATHER ANNOUNCING THE WORLD'S FIRST POWERED FLIGHT, DECEMBER 17, 1903

The world must be made safe for democracy.

PRESIDENT WOODROW WILSON, IN SPEECH TO CONGRESS REQUEST-ING A DECLARATION OF WAR AGAINST GERMANY, APRIL 2, 1917

The right of citizens of the United States to vote shall
not be denied or abridged by the United States or by
any State on account of sex.

THE NINETEENTH AMENDMENT TO THE UNITED STATES
CONSTITUTION, RATIFIED ON AUGUST 26, 1920

I live only in the moment in this strange unmortal
space, crowded with beauty, pierced with danger.

CHARLES A. LINDBERGH, *SPIRIT OF ST. LOUIS* (1953)

Wall St. Lays an Egg

SIME SILVERMAN, HEADLINE ANNOUNCING STOCK MARKET CRASH,
VARIETY, OCTOBER 30, 1929

———◦————

I pledge you—I pledge myself to a new deal for the American people.

FRANKLIN D. ROOSEVELT, ACCEPTANCE SPEECH AT DEMOCRATIC
NATIONAL CONVENTION, 1932

Yesterday, December 7, 1941—a date that will live in infamy—the United States of America was suddenly and deliberately attacked by naval and air forces of the Empire of Japan.

FRANKLIN D. ROOSEVELT, ADDRESS TO CONGRESS REQUESTING DECLARATION OF WAR AGAINST JAPAN, DECEMBER 8, 1941

The eyes of the world are upon you. The hopes and prayers of liberty-loving people everywhere march with you.

GENERAL DWIGHT D. EISENHOWER, ORDER TO HIS TROOPS ON D-DAY, JUNE 6, 1944

They've got us surrounded again, the poor bastards.

GENERAL CREIGHTON W. ABRAMS JR., U.S. ARMY, DURING THE
BATTLE OF THE BULGE

———•◦•———

The flags of freedom fly all over Europe.

HARRY S TRUMAN, VE-DAY, MAY 8, 1945

Babies satisfactorily born.

CODED MESSAGE INDICATING THAT AN ATOMIC BOMB HAD BEEN
SUCCESSFULLY EXPLODED, JULY 1945

———

As the bomb fell over Hiroshima and exploded, we saw an entire city disappear. I wrote in my log the words: "My God, what have we done?"

CAPTAIN ROBERT LEWIS, U.S. ARMY AIR CORPS, COPILOT OF THE
ENOLA GAY

Let us not be deceived—we are today in the midst of a cold war.

BERNARD BARUCH, UNITED STATES FINANCIER, IN SPEECH TO THE SOUTH CAROLINA LEGISLATURE, APRIL 16, 1947

While I cannot take the time to name all of the men in the State Department who have been named as members of the Communist Party and members of a spy ring, I have here in my hand a list of 205 that were known to the Secretary of State

SENATOR JOSEPH R. MCCARTHY, SPEECH THAT BEGAN HIS CAMPAIGN AGAINST ALLEGED COMMUNISTS IN THE GOVERNMENT AND ELSE-WHERE, FEBRUARY 9, 1950

The attack upon Korea makes it plain beyond all doubt that Communism has passed beyond the use of subversion to conquer independent nations, and will now use armed invasion and war.

PRESIDENT HARRY S TRUMAN, JUNE 27, 1950

I return with feelings of misgiving from my third war—I was the first American commander to put his signature to a paper ending a war when we did not win it.

GENERAL MARK W. CLARK, U.S. ARMY, RETIRING AS COMMANDER OF UN FORCES IN KOREA, *THE NEW YORK HERALD TRIBUNE*, OCTOBER 21, 1953

Separate educational facilities are inherently un-equal.

EARL WARREN, UNANIMOUS OPINION OF THE SUPREME COURT IN BROWN V. BOARD OF EDUCATION OF TOPEKA, MAY 17, 1954

Until this moment, Senator, I think I had never gauged your cruelty or your recklessness. Have you no sense of decency, sir, at long last? Have you left no sense of decency?

JOSEPH N. WELCH, TO SENATOR JOSEPH J. MCCARTHY, JUNE 9, 1954

All I was doing was trying to get home from work.

ROSA PARKS, ON REFUSING TO GIVE UP HER SEAT TO A WHITE MAN
AND MOVE TO THE BACK OF A BUS, A MOVE THAT SPARKED THE CIVIL-
RIGHTS MOVEMENT

Whether you like it or not, history is on our side. We will bury you.

NIKITA KHRUSHCHEV, SOVIET PREMIER, REMARK TO WESTERN
DIPLOMATS, NOVEMBER 18, 1956

A-OK full go.

ALAN SHEPARD, THE FIRST AMERICAN IN SPACE, DURING BLASTOFF,
MAY 5, 1961

The path we have chosen for the present is full of hazards, as all paths are. The cost of freedom is always high, but Americans have always paid it. And one path we shall never choose, and that is the path of surrender.

JOHN F. KENNEDY, ANNOUNCING U.S. BLOCKADE OF CUBA,
AFTER INSTALLATION OF SOVIET MISSILES, OCTOBER 22, 1962

I have a dream that one day on the red hills of Georgia, the sons of former slaves and the sons of former slave owners will be able to sit together at the table of brotherhood.

MARTIN LUTHER KING, JR., AUGUST 28, 1963

It all began so beautifully. After a drizzle in the morning, the sun came out bright and clear. We were driving into Dallas. In the lead car were President and Mrs. Kennedy.

NOVEMBER 22, 1963, AS RECALLED BY LADY BIRD JOHNSON, WIFE OF LYNDON BAINES JOHNSON, *A WHITE HOUSE DIARY* (1970)

Mr. Speaker, Mr. President, Members of the House, Members of the Senate, my fellow Americans, all I have I would have given gladly not to be standing here today.

LYNDON BAINES JOHNSON, IN FIRST SPEECH TO CONGRESS AS PRESIDENT, NOVEMBER 27, 1963

I thought they'd get one of us, but Jack, after all he's been through, never worried about it. I thought it would be me.

ROBERT F. KENNEDY, UPON LEARNING OF HIS OLDER BROTHER'S DEATH

We are not about to send American boys nine or ten thousand miles away from home to do what Asian boys ought to be doing for themselves.

LYNDON BAINES JOHNSON, OCTOBER 21, 1964

They've got to draw in their horns and stop their aggression, or we're going to bomb them back into the Stone Age.

GENERAL CURTIS E. LEMAY, U.S. AIR FORCE, *MISSION WITH LEMAY: MY STORY* (1965)

That's one small step for [a] man, one giant leap
for mankind.

NEIL A. ARMSTRONG, JULY 20, 1969

We, therefore, conclude that the right of personal
privacy includes the abortion decision, but that this
right is not unqualified.

HARRY A. BLACKMUN, IN *ROE V. WADE*, THE DECISION THAT ESTAB-
LISHED THE LEGALITY OF ABORTION, JANUARY 22, 1973

I have never been a quitter. To leave office before my term is completed is opposed to every instinct in my body. But as president I must put the interests of America first. Therefore, I shall resign the presidency effective at noon tomorrow.

RICHARD M. NIXON, AUGUST 8, 1974

In the end, we simply cut and ran. The American national will had collapsed.

GRAHAM A. MARTIN, FORMER AMBASSADOR TO SOUTH VIETNAM, RECALLING THE FALL OF SAIGON ON THE TENTH ANNIVERSARY, *THE NEW YORK TIMES*, APRIL 30, 1985

Vader was seduced by the dark side of the Force.

OBI WAN KENOBI (ALEC GUINESS), *STAR WARS*, 1977

———•••———

The rescuers had to rescue themselves

TIME MAGAZINE, ON THE ILL-FATED ATTEMPT TO RESCUE HOSTAGES
HELD AT THE AMERICAN EMBASSY IN TEHRAN, MAY 5, 1980

Please tell me you're Republicans.

RONALD REAGAN, TO SURGEONS AS HE ENTERED OPERATING ROOM
AFTER BEING SHOT IN AN ASSASSINATION ATTEMPT, MARCH 30, 1981

Obviously a major malfunction.

STEPHEN NESBITT, NASA PUBLIC AFFAIRS OFFICER, ANNOUNCE-
MENT MADE JUST AFTER THE SPACE SHUTTLE *CHALLENGER* EXPLODED
ON JANUARY 28, 1986

General Secretary Gorbachev, if you seek peace, if you seek prosperity for the Soviet Union and Eastern Europe, if you seek liberalization: Come here to this gate! Mr. Gorbachev, open this gate! Mr. Gorbachev, tear down this wall!"

RONALD REAGAN, IN SPEECH DELIVERED NEAR THE BERLIN WALL, JUNE 12, 1987

They came, they saw, they did a little shopping

GRAFFITI ON THE BERLIN WALL AFTER THOUSANDS OF EAST BERLINERS POURED INTO WEST BERLIN, REPORTED IN NEWSWEEK, DECEMBER 4, 1989

Just two hours ago, allied air forces began an attack on military targets in Iraq and Kuwait. These attacks continue as I speak.

GEORGE H. W. BUSH, JANUARY 16, 1991

I'm absolutely, 100 percent, not guilty.

O. J. (ORENTHAL JAMES) SIMPSON

My first glimpse of the actual building left me speechless. I was dumbfounded. I was looking at it, but still not believing it, as if it were just some clever bit of matte painting in a George Lucas film.

OMAR GALLAGA, REPORTER, ON SURVEYING THE RUINS OF THE ALFRED P. MURRAH FEDERAL BUILDING IN OKLAHOMA CITY, APRIL 19, 1995

All the pigeons in the street flew up.

A NEW YORKER DESCRIBING THE SOUND OF A JET PASSING TOO LOW OVERHEAD, SEPTEMBER 11, 2001, QUOTED IN THE NEW YORK TIMES

The city is going to survive, we are going to get through it. It's going to be very, very difficult time. I don't think we yet know the pain that we're going to feel when we find out who we lost, but the thing we have to focus on now is getting this city through this, and surviving and being stronger for it.

RUDOLPH W. GIULIANI, MAYOR OF NEW YORK CITY, SEPTEMBER 11, 2001

Thousands of lives were suddenly ended by evil, despicable acts of terror. The pictures of airplanes flying into buildings, fires burning, huge structures collapsing have filled us with disbelief, terrible sadness, and a quiet, unyielding anger.

PRESIDENT GEORGE W. BUSH, SPEECH MADE FROM THE OVAL OFFICE ON THE EVENING OF SEPTEMBER 11, 2001

Great tragedy has come to us, and we are meeting it with the best that is in our country, with courage and concern for others. Because this is America. This is who we are.

PRESIDENT GEORGE W. BUSH, SEPTEMBER 15, 2001

Sea to Shining Sea:
The American Landscape

This continent, an open palm spread frank before the sky.

JAMES AGEE, 1954

⸺•⸺

America was too big to have been discovered all at one time. It would have been better for the graces if it had been discovered in pieces of about the size of France or Germany at a time.

SAMUEL BUTLER, BRITISH AUTHOR, 1912, *SAMUEL BUTLER'S NOTEBOOKS* (1951)

New York is to the nation what the white church spire is to the village—the visible symbol of aspiration and faith, the white plume saying the way is up!

E. B. WHITE, "HERE IS NEW YORK," IN *HOLIDAY* MAGAZINE, 1949

I shall enter on no encomium upon Massachusetts; she needs none. There she is. Behold her, and judge for yourselves. There is her history; the world knows it by heart. There is Boston and Concord and Lexington and Bunker Hill; and there they will remain forever.

DANIEL WEBSTER, SECOND SPEECH ON FOOT'S RESOLUTION, JANUARY 26, 1830

We say the cows laid out Boston. Well, there are worse surveyors.

RALPH WALDO EMERSON, "WEALTH," IN *THE CONDUCT OF LIFE* (1860)

There is a sumptuous variety about the New England weather that compels the stranger's admiration—and regret. The weather is always doing something there; always attending strictly to business; always getting up new designs and trying them on people to see how they will go. In the Spring I have counted one hundred and thirty-six different kinds of weather inside of twenty-four hours.

MARK TWAIN, IN "NEW ENGLAND WEATHER," 1876

A storm in the fall or winter is the time to visit it; a lighthouse or fisherman's hut, the true hotel. A man may stand there and put all America behind him.

HENRY DAVID THOREAU, *CAPE COD* (1855–1865)

From space Baja resembles the languorously splayed leg of some great earth mother, from whose womb pours the Colorado River and its cargo of eroded continental spine, nourishment for the fertile sea of Cortez.

JAMES R. BABB, "CABO WABO," *CROSSCURRENTS* (1999)

I was disappointed in Niagara—most people must be disappointed in Niagara. Every American bride is taken there, and the sight of the stupendous waterfall must be one of the earliest, if not the keenest, disappointments in American married life.

OSCAR WILDE, ENGLISH-IRISH AUTHOR, "PERSONAL IMPRESSIONS OF AMERICA," 1883

As a nation, we are the children of those who tried to solve old problems with a new place, and that may be why the first writing about America comes from explorers and why other travelers' accounts have flourished for half a millennium.

WILLIAM LEAST HEAT-MOON, *BLUE HIGHWAYS* (1982)

Philadelphia, the home of respectability, and the city of respectable homes.

ANONYMOUS

A state that has three counties when the tide is out, and two when it is in.

JOHN J. INGALLS, DESCRIBING DELAWARE, SPEECH IN THE U.S. SENATE, CIRCA 1885

Never again, I vowed, would I try to hike the Appalachian Trail by car.

BILL BRYSON, *A WALK IN THE WOODS* (1998)

Heaven and earth never agreed to frame a better place for man's habitation.

JOHN SMITH, DESCRIBING CHESAPEAKE BAY AS HE FOUND IT IN 1607

Washington is a city of Southern efficiency and Northern charm.

JOHN F. KENNEDY, NOVEMBER 1961

North Carolina is a valley of humility between two mountains of conceit.

ANONYMOUS

The average Southerner has the speech patterns of someone slipping in and out of consciousness. I can change my shoes and socks faster than most people in Mississippi can speak a sentence.

BILL BRYSON, *THE LOST CONTINENT: TRAVELS IN SMALL TOWN AMERICA* (1989)

No people require maxims so much as the American. The reason is obvious: the country is so vast, the people always going somewhere, from Oregon apple valley to boreal New England, that we do not know whether to be temperate orchards or sterile climate.

EDWARD DAHLBERG, *ALMS FOR OBLIVION* (1964)

The state with the prettiest name,
the state that floats in brackish water,
held together by mangrove roots.

ELIZABETH BISHOP, "FLORIDA," (1939)

A resistless feeling of depression falls slowly upon us, despite the gaudy sunshine and the green cotton-fields. This, then, is the Cotton Kingdom, the shadow of a marvelous dream.

W. E. B. DUBOIS, *THE SOULS OF BLACK FOLK* (1903)

The thousands of warblers and thrushes, the richly blossoming magnolias, the holly, beech, tall yellow poplar, red clay earth, and hill ground delighted my eye.

JOHN JAMES AUDUBON, ORNITHOLOGIST AND PAINTER, DESCRIBING LOUISIANA, JOURNAL, 1820

I was never lost, but I was bewildered once for three days.

DANIEL BOONE

The songbirds are the sweetest
In Kentucky;
The thoroughbreds are fleetest
In Kentucky;
Mountains tower proudest,
Thunder peals the loudest
The landscape is the grandest—
And the politics—the damnedest
In Kentucky

JAMES HILARY MULLIGAN, "IN KENTUCKY," (1902)

The interstate highway system is a wonderful thing. It makes it possible to go coast to coast without seeing anything or meeting anybody.

CHARLES KURALT, *A LIFE ON THE ROAD*

———

Ohio is the farthest west of the east and the farthest north of the south.

LOUIS BROMFIELD, *THE TRAVELLER'S DICTIONARY OF QUOTATIONS* (1983)

Michigan is the skyscraper, the mass-production line, and the frantic rush into what the machine will someday make of us, and at the same time, it is golden sand, blue water, green pine trees on empty hills, and a wind that comes down from the cold spaces, scented with the forests.

BRUCE CATTON, *AMERICAN PANORAMA, EAST OF THE MISSISSIPPI* (1960)

Over increasingly large areas of the United States, spring now comes unheralded by the return of the birds, and the early mornings are strangely silent.

RACHEL CARSON, *SILENT SPRING* (1962)

New York is one of the capitals of the world and Los Angeles is a constellation of plastic, San Francisco is a lady, Boston has become Urban Renewal, Philadelphia and Baltimore and Washington blink like dull diamonds in the smog of Eastern Megalopolis. But Chicago is a great American city.

NORMAN MAILER, *MIAMI AND THE SIEGE OF CHICAGO* (1969)

I had sneaked into San Francisco . . . coming 3,000 miles . . . in a pleasant roomette on the California Zephyr train watching America roll by outside my private picture window. . . . all so easy and dreamlike compared to my old harsh hitch hiking before I made enough money to take transcontinental trains.

JACK KEROUAC, *BIG SUR* (1962)

When we get piled upon one another in large cities as in Europe, we shall become corrupt as in Europe, and go to eating one another as they do there.

THOMAS JEFFERSON, LETTER TO JAMES MADISON, DECEMBER 20, 1787

Other nations have tried to check the fulfillment of our manifest destiny to overspread the continent allotted by Providence for the free development of our yearly multiplying millions.

JOHN LOUIS O'SULLIVAN, *U.S. MAGAZINE & DEMOCRATIC REVIEW*, 1845

Go West, young man, and grow up with the country.

HORACE GREELEY, NEWSPAPER EDITOR, *HINTS TOWARD REFORMS* (1850)

There seemed to be nothing to see; no fences, no creeks or trees, no hills or fields. If there was a road, I could not make it out in the faint starlight. There was nothing but land: not a country at all, but the material out of which countries are made.

WILLA CATHER, *MY ANTONIA* (1918)

These are the gardens of the desert, these
The unshorn fields, boundless and beautiful,
For which the speech of England has no name—
The prairies.

WILLIAM CULLEN BRYANT, *THE PRAIRIES* (1833)

In the United States there is more space where nobody is than where anybody is. That is what makes America what it is.

GERTRUDE STEIN, *THE GEOGRAPHICAL HISTORY OF AMERICA* (1936)

The country before us thronged with buffalo. They were crowded so densely together that in the distance their rounded backs presented a surface of uniform blackness.

FRANCIS PARKMAN, *THE OREGON TRAIL* (1847)

If a Maine winter is nothing else, it is prime time for brooding over life's inherent inequities, a fertile incubator of unrealized expectations.

JAMES R. BABB, *RIVER MUSIC* (2001)

What you Kansas farmers ought to do is raise less corn and more hell.

MARY ELIZABETH LEASE, WRITER AND AGRARIAN REFORMER, SPEECH, 1890

Where all the women are strong, all the men are good-looking, and all the children are above-average.

GARRISON KEILLOR, ON LAKE WOBEGON

I was not prepared for the Bad Lands. They deserve this name. They are like the work of an evil child.

JOHN STEINBECK, DESCRIBING SOUTH DAKOTA, *TRAVELS WITH CHARLEY: IN SEARCH OF AMERICA* (1962)

In Houston the air was warm and rich and suggestive of fossil fuel.

JOHN GUNTHER, *INSIDE U.S.A.* (1947)

They were most wonderful against the blue—that blue that will always be there as it is now after all man's destruction is finished.

GEORGIA O'KEEFFE, AMERICAN PAINTER, DESCRIBING BLEACHED BONES AND THE DESERT SKIES OF NEW MEXICO, *NEWSWEEK*, MARCH 17, 1986

I take SPACE to be the central fact to man born in America. I spell it large because it comes large here. Large and without mercy.

CHARLES OLSON, *CALL ME ISHMAEL* (1947)

———

Across the Colorado River from Needles, the dark and jagged ramparts of Arizona stood up against the sky, and behind them the huge tilted plain rising toward the backbone of the continent again.

JOHN STEINBECK, *TRAVELS WITH CHARLEY: IN SEARCH OF AMERICA* (1962)

Nevada—it's freedom's last stand in America.

WILL ROGERS, *THE WIT AND WISDOM OF WILL ROGERS* (1993)

———

This is the place!

BRIGHAM YOUNG, UPON SIGHTING THE GREAT SALT LAKE VALLEY,
JULY 24, 1847

About the only thing that will make a Wyoming cattleman reach for his gun nowadays is to call him a "farmer." A "rancher," he wants it clearly understood, drinks only canned milk, never eats vegetables, and grows nothing but hay and whiskers.

JOHN GUNTHER, *INSIDE U.S.A.* (1947)

Yosemite Valley, to me, is always a sunrise, a glitter of green and golden wonder in a vast edifice of stone and space.

ANSEL ADAMS, *THE PORTFOLIOS OF ANSEL ADAMS* (1981)

The clearest way into the universe is through a forest wilderness.

JOHN MUIR, *JOHN OF THE MOUNTAINS* (1938)

A hundred miles of traveling on water, and I was ready for a rest.

PETER JENKINS, *ALONG THE EDGE OF AMERICA* (1995)

Dice 'em, hash 'em, boil 'em, mash 'em!
Idaho, Idaho, Idaho!

ANONYMOUS, FOOTBALL CHEER, QUOTED BY CHARLES KURALT,
DATELINE AMERICA (1979)

The miners came in forty-nine;
The whores in fifty-one;
And when they got together
They produced the native son.

ANONYMOUS SONG, 1850S

This valley is a paradise. Grass, flowers, trees, beautiful clear rivers, thousands of deer, elk, wild horses, wonderful salmon, thousands of different kinds of ducks here; geese standing around as if tame.

CHARLES PREUSS, DESCRIBING THE SAN JOAQUIN VALLEY, MARCH 27, 1844, *EXPLORING WITH FREMONT* (1958)

California is a fine place to live—if you happen to be an orange.

FRED ALLEN, COMEDIAN, *AMERICAN MAGAZINE* (DECEMBER, 1945)

Santa Barbara is a paradise; Disneyland is a paradise; the U.S. is a paradise. Paradise is just paradise. Mournful, monotonous, and superficial though it may be, it is paradise. There is no other.

JEAN BAUDRILLARD, FRENCH PHILOSOPHER, "UTOPIA ACHIEVED," *AMERICA* (1986)

Rainier, from Puget Sound, is a sight for the gods, and when one looks upon him he feels that he is in the presence of the gods.

PAUL FOUNTAIN, *THE ELEVEN EAGLETS OF THE WEST* (1905)

In the making of the world God grew tired, and when He came to the last barrowload, "just dumped it anyhow," and that was how Alaska happened to be.

JACK LONDON, ON LIFE IN ALASKA, "GOLD HUNTERS OF THE NORTH," IN *REVOLUTION AND OTHER ESSAYS* (1910)

For me its balmy airs are always blowing, its summer seas flashing in the sun; the pulsing of its surf-beat in my ear; I can see its garlanded crags, its leaping cascades, its plumy palms drowsing by the shore; its remote summits floating like islands above the cloud rack

MARK TWAIN, DESCRIBING HAWAII, *PARADISE OF THE PACIFIC* (1910)

This monster of a land, this mightiest of nations, this spawn of the future, turns out to be the macrocosm of microcosm me.

JOHN STEINBECK, *TRAVELS WITH CHARLEY: IN SEARCH OF AMERICA* (1962)

Democracy

The republic is a dream.
Nothing happens unless first a dream.

CARL SANDBURG, *WASHINGTON MONUMENT BY NIGHT* (1922)

They that can give up essential liberty to obtain a little temporary safety deserve neither liberty nor safety.

BENJAMIN FRANKLIN, SPEECH, NOVEMBER 11, 1755

We hold these truths to be self-evident, that all men are created equal, that they are endowed by their Creator with certain unalienable rights, that among these are life, liberty, and the pursuit of happiness.

THOMAS JEFFERSON, AMERICAN DECLARATION OF INDEPENDENCE (1776)

Man's capacity for evil makes democracy necessary, and man's capacity for good makes democracy possible.

REINHOLD NIEBUHR, AMERICAN THEOLOGIAN

The surface of American society is covered with a layer of democratic paint, but from time to time one can see the old aristocratic colors breaking through.

ALEXIS DE TOCQUEVILLE, *DEMOCRACY IN AMERICA* (1835–1840)

———•••———

The tendency of democracy is, in all things, to mediocrity.

JAMES FENIMORE COOPER, *THE AMERICAN DEMOCRAT* (1838)

Remember, democracy never lasts long. It soon wastes, exhausts, and murders itself. There never was a democracy yet that did not commit suicide.

JOHN ADAMS, SECOND PRESIDENT, LETTER, APRIL 15, 1814

Were it left to me to decide whether we should have a government without newspapers, or newspapers without a government, I should not hesitate a moment to prefer the latter.

THOMAS JEFFERSON, LETTER, JANUARY 16, 1787

Congress shall make no law respecting an establishment of religion, or prohibiting the free exercise thereof; or abridging the freedom of speech or of the press; or the right of the people peaceably to assemble, and to petition the government for a redress of grievances.

AMENDMENT I OF THE UNITED STATES CONSTITUTION

The constant aim is to divide and arrange the several offices in such a manner as that each may be a check on the other—that the private interest of every individual may be a sentinel over the public rights.

JAMES MADISON, DESCRIBING THE ENGINEERING OF GOVERNMENT, *THE FEDERALIST*, NO. 51 (1788)

The American Constitution, one of the few modern political documents drawn up by men who were forced by the sternest circumstances to think out what they really had to face instead of chopping logic in a university classroom.

GEORGE BERNARD SHAW, *GETTING MARRIED* (1911)

To live under the American Constitution is the greatest political privilege that was ever accorded to the human race.

ATTRIBUTED TO CALVIN COOLIDGE (1924)

I confess that there are several parts of this Constitution which I do not at present approve, but I am not sure I shall never approve them.

BENJAMIN FRANKLIN, SPEECH IN THE CONSTITUTIONAL CONVENTION, SEPTEMBER 17, 1787

Our Constitution is so simple and practical that it is possible always to meet extraordinary needs by changes in emphasis and arrangement without loss of simple form.

FRANKLIN D. ROOSEVELT, FIRST INAUGURAL ADDRESS, MARCH 4, 1933

The Constitution is what the judges say it is.

CHARLES EVANS HUGHES, SPEECH, 1907

———•••———

The makers of our Constitution conferred, as against the Government, the right to be let alone—the most comprehensive of rights and the right most valued by civilized men.

LOUIS D. BRANDEIS, *OLMSTEAD V. U.S.*, DISSENTING OPINION, 1928

There is more law in the end of a policeman's night-stick than in a decision of the Supreme Court.

ALEXANDER S. WILLIAMS, ATTRIBUTED C. 1870

No man is good enough to govern another man without that other's consent.

ABRAHAM LINCOLN, SPEECH, 1854

Freedom is never given; it is won.

A. PHILIP RANDOLPH, KEYNOTE SPEECH AT THE SECOND NATIONAL NEGRO CONGRESS, 1937

It is high time that the women of Republican America should know how much the laws that govern them are like the slave laws of the South.

HARRIOT K. HUNT, PHYSICIAN AND FEMINIST, *GLANCES AND GLIMPSES* (1856)

Neither slavery nor involuntary servitude, except as a punishment for crime whereof the party shall have been duly convicted, shall exist within the United States, or any place subject to their jurisdiction.

AMENDMENT XIII OF THE UNITED STATES CONSTITUTION, RATIFIED 1865

Anglo-Saxon civilization has taught the individual to protect his own rights; American civilization will teach him to respect the rights of others.

WILLIAM JENNINGS BRYAN, DEMOCRATIC POLITICIAN, SPEECH, 1899

When we shall have our amendment to the Constitution of the United States, everyone will think it was always so, just exactly as many young people believe that all the privileges, all the freedom, all the enjoyments which woman now possesses were always hers. They have no idea of how every single inch of ground that she stands upon to-day has been gained by the hard work of some little handful of women of the past.

SUSAN B. ANTHONY, IN *HISTORY OF WOMAN SUFFRAGE* (1902)

None who have always been free can understand the terrible fascinating power of the hope of freedom to those who are not free.

PEARL S. BUCK, *WHAT AMERICA MEANS TO ME* (1943)

Democracy is the recurrent suspicion that more than half of the people are right more than half of the time.

E. B. WHITE, *THE NEW YORKER*, JULY 3, 1944

One fifth of the people are against everything all the time.

ROBERT F. KENNEDY, 1964

The natural progress of things is for liberty to yield and government to gain ground.

THOMAS JEFFERSON, LETTER TO COL. EDWARD CARRINGTON, 1788

A majority can do anything.

REPRESENTATIVE JOSEPH G. CANNON, SPEAKER OF THE HOUSE FROM
1903 TO 1911

———•••———

No government is ever perfect. One of the chief
virtues of a democracy, however, is that its defects are
always visible and under democratic processes can be
pointed out and corrected.

HARRY S TRUMAN, 1947

The spirit of resistance to government is so valuable on certain occasions that I wish it to be always kept alive. It will often be exercised when wrong, but better so than not to be exercised at all.

THOMAS JEFFERSON, LETTER TO ABIGAIL ADAMS, FEBRUARY 22, 1787

Discussion in America means dissent.

JAMES THURBER, *LANTERNS AND LANCES* (1961)

I say violence is necessary. Violence is as American as cherry pie.

H. RAP BROWN, 1967

Every actual State is corrupt. Good men must not obey the laws too well.

RALPH WALDO EMERSON, "POLITICS," *ESSAYS, SECOND SERIES,* 1844

Under a government which imprisons any unjustly,
the true place for a just man is also a prison.

HENRY DAVID THOREAU, *CIVIL DISOBEDIENCE* (1849)

———

Injustice anywhere is a threat to justice everywhere.

MARTIN LUTHER KING JR., "LETTER FROM BIRMINGHAM JAIL,"
APRIL 16, 1963

A citizen of America will cross the ocean to fight for democracy but won't cross the street to vote in a national election.

BILL VAUGHAN

Nothing would please the Kremlin more than to have the people of this country choose a second-rate president.

RICHARD M. NIXON

The cure for the evils of democracy is more democracy.

H. L. MENCKEN, *NOTES ON DEMOCRACY* (1926)

I believe in the United States of America as a government of the people, by the people, for the people, whose just powers are derived from the consent of the governed; a democracy in a republic; a sovereign Nation of many sovereign States; a perfect Union, one and inseparable

WILLIAM TYLER PAGE, *AMERICAN'S CREED* (1918)

The Melting Pot

America is God's Crucible, the great Melting-Pot where all the races of Europe are melting and reforming! Germans and Frenchmen, Irishmen and Englishmen, Jews and Russians—into the crucible with you all! God is making the American!

ISRAEL ZANGWILL, BRITISH PLAYWRIGHT, *THE MELTING POT,* 1908

The bosom of America is open to receive not only the Opulent and respectable Stranger, but the oppressed and persecuted of all Nations and Religions; whom we shall welcome to a participation of all our rights and privileges, if by decency and propriety of conduct they appear to merit the enjoyment.

GEORGE WASHINGTON, 1783

America was indebted to immigration for her settlement and prosperity. That part of America which had
encouraged them most had advanced most rapidly in
population, agriculture, and the arts.

JAMES MADISON, SPEECH AT FEDERAL CONVENTION, AUGUST 13,
1787

Before the Pilgrims landed at Plymouth, we were
here. Before the pen of Jefferson etched across the
pages of history the majestic words of the
Declaration of Independence, we were here.

MARTIN LUTHER KING JR., ADDRESS AT BIRMINGHAM, 1963

The destiny of the colored America is the destiny of America.

FREDERICK DOUGLASS, SPEECH, EMANCIPATION LEAGUE, BOSTON, 1862

The danger of a conflict between the white and the black inhabitants perpetually haunts the imagination of the Americans like a bad dream.

ALEXIS DE TOCQUEVILLE, *DEMOCRACY IN AMERICA* (1835)

Their name is on your water—
Ye may not wash it out.

LYDIA HUNTLEY SIGOURNEY, *INDIAN NAMES*, 1841

When the last red man shall have vanished from this earth, and his memory is only a story among the whites, these shores will still swarm with the invisible dead of my people.

SEATTLE, C. 1854

Give me your tired, your poor,
Your huddled masses yearning to breathe free,
The wretched refuse of your teeming shore,
Send these, the homeless, tempest-tossed to me,
I lift my lamp beside the golden door!

EMMA LAZARUS, AMERICAN POET, "THE NEW COLOSSUS," 1886

America has been another name for opportunity.

FREDERICK J. TURNER, *THE SIGNIFICANCE OF THE FRONTIER IN
AMERICAN HISTORY* (1893)

America thou half-brother of the world!
With something good and bad of every land.

PHILIP JAMES BAILEY, *FESTUS*

There is no king who has not had a slave among his
ancestors, and no slave who has not had a king among
his.

HELEN KELLER, *THE STORY OF MY LIFE* (1903)

You cannot become thorough Americans if you think of yourselves in groups. America does not consist of groups. A man who thinks of himself as belonging to a particular national group in America has not yet become an American.

WOODROW WILSON, SPEECH, 1915

Americans are impatient with memory.

JAMAICA KINCAID, "ALIEN SOIL," *THE NEW YORKER*, JUNE 21, 1993

Remember always that all of us, and you and I especially, are descended from immigrants and revolutionists.

FRANKLIN D. ROOSEVELT, REMARKS TO THE DAUGHTERS OF THE AMERICAN REVOLUTION, 1938

America has believed that in differentiation, not in uniformity, lies the path of progress. It acted on this belief; it has advanced human happiness, and it has prospered.

LOUIS D. BRANDEIS, ASSOCIATE JUSTICE OF THE SUPREME COURT

Without comprehension, the immigrant would forever remain shut—a stranger in America. Until America can release the heart as well as train the hand of the immigrant, he would forever remain driven back upon himself, corroded by the very richness of the unused gifts within his soul.

ANZIA YEZIERSKA, *HOW I FOUND AMERICA* (1920)

The great social adventure of America is no longer the conquest of the wilderness but the absorption of fifty different peoples.

WALTER LIPPMANN, AMERICAN JOURNALIST, *POLITICS* (1914)

One ever feels his twoness—an American, a Negro; two souls, two thoughts, two unreconciled strivings; two warring ideals in one dark body, whose dogged strength alone keeps it from being torn asunder.

W. E. B. DuBois, *THE SOULS OF BLACK FOLK* (1903)

Among the thousand white persons, I am a dark rock surged upon, and overswept.

ZORA NEALE HURSTON, *MULES AND MEN* (1935)

It is not healthy when a nation lives within a nation, as colored Americans are living inside America. A nation cannot live confident of its tomorrow if its refugees are among its own citizens.

PEARL S. BUCK, *WHAT AMERICAN MEANS TO ME* (1942)

Melting pot Harlem—Harlem of honey and chocolate and caramel and rum and vinegar and lemon and lime and gall.

LANGSTON HUGHES, "IN LOVE WITH HARLEM," 1963

I have a dream that my four little children will one day live in a nation where they will not be judged by the color of their skin, but by the content of their character.

MARTIN LUTHER KING JR., ADDRESS AT LINCOLN MEMORIAL, MARCH ON WASHINGTON, AUGUST 28, 1963

This nation is founded
  on blood like a city on swamps
yet its dream has been
  beautiful and sometimes just

MARGE PIERCY, AMERICAN WRITER, "THE PEACEABLE KINGDOM"
(1968)

It's time for America to get right.

FANNIE LOU HAMER, CIVIL RIGHTS ACTIVIST, 1965

I am America. I am the part you won't recognize. But get used to me. Black, confident, cocky; my name, not yours; my religion, not yours; my goals, my own; get used to me.

MUHAMMAD ALI, *THE GREATEST* (1975)

Ultimately, America's answer to the intolerant man is diversity, the very diversity which our heritage of religious freedom has inspired.

ROBERT F. KENNEDY, *THE PURSUIT OF JUSTICE* (1964)

I hope that no American will waste his franchise and throw away his vote by voting either for me or against me solely on account of my religious affiliation. It is not relevant.

JOHN F. KENNEDY, REFERRING TO HIS CATHOLICISM, *TIME*, JULY 25, 1960

＊

We become not a melting pot but a beautiful mosaic. Different people, different beliefs, different yearnings, different hopes, different dreams.

JIMMY CARTER, 1976

Tell me this—where in Europe can you find old Hungary, old Russia, old France, old Italy? In Europe you're trying to copy America, you're almost American. But here you'll find Europeans who immigrated a hundred years ago—and we haven't spoiled them.

ORIANA FALLACI, PRAISING NEW YORK CITY, *PENELOPE AT WAR* (1966)

The aspiring immigrant is not content to progress alone. Solitary success is imperfect success in his eyes. He must take his family with him as he rises.

MARY ANTIN, *THE PROMISED LAND* (1912)

People, when they first come to America, whether as travelers or settlers, become aware of a new and agreeable feeling: that the whole country is their oyster.

ALISTAIR COOKE, *AMERICA* (1973)

My mother believed you could be anything you wanted to be in America. You could open a restaurant. You could work for the government and get good retirement. You could buy a house with almost no money down. You could become rich. You could become instantly famous.

AMY TAN, *THE JOY LUCK CLUB* (1989)

Only in America could a refugee girl from Europe become Secretary of State.

MADELEINE ALBRIGHT, 1998

His foreparents came to America in immigrant ships. My foreparents came to America in slave ships. But whatever the original ships, we are both in the same boat tonight.

JESSE JACKSON, 1988

American means white, and Africanist people struggle to make the term applicable to themselves with ethnicity and hyphen after hyphen after hyphen.

TONI MORRISON, *PLAYING IN THE DARK: WHITENESS AND THE LITERARY IMAGINATION* (1992)

Whoever the last true cowboy in America turns out to be, he's likely to be an Indian.

WILLIAM LEAST HEAT-MOON, *BLUE HIGHWAYS: A JOURNEY INTO AMERICA* (1983)

There is nothing wrong with America that cannot be cured by what is right with America.

BILL CLINTON, INAUGURAL ADDRESS, JANUARY 20, 1993

America is not like a blanket—one piece of unbroken cloth, the same color, the same texture, the same size. America is more like a quilt—many patches, many pieces, many colors, many sizes, all woven and held together by a common thread.

JESSE JACKSON, SPEECH AT THE DEMOCRATIC NATIONAL CONVENTION, 1984

Politics

Our Constitution is in actual operation; everything appears to promise that it will last; but in this world nothing is certain but death and taxes.

BENJAMIN FRANKLIN, LETTER, 1789

The political activity prevailing in the United States is something one could never understand unless one had seen it. No sooner do you set foot on American soil than you find yourself in a sort of tumult; a confused clamor rises on every side, and a thousand voices are heard at once, each expressing some social requirements.

ALEXIS DE TOCQUEVILLE, *DEMOCRACY IN AMERICA* (1835–1840)

There is no excitement anywhere in the world, short of war, to match the excitement of an American presidential campaign.

THEODORE H. WHITE

PRESIDENCY, n. The greased pig in the field game of American politics.

AMBROSE BIERCE, *THE DEVIL'S DICTIONARY* (1906)

My God! What is there in this place that a man should ever want to get into it?

JAMES A. GARFIELD, DIARY ENTRY, JUNE 8, 1881

He'll sit right here and he'll say do this, do that! And nothing will happen. Poor Ike—it won't be a bit like the Army.

HARRY S TRUMAN, IMAGINING EISENHOWER, HIS SUCCESSOR, AS PRESIDENT, 1952

I will not accept if nominated, and will not serve if elected.

WILLIAM T. SHERMAN, AMERICAN CIVIL WAR GENERAL, RESPOND-
ING TO A REQUEST TO RUN AS THE REPUBLICAN PRESIDENTIAL CAN-
DIDATE IN 1884

My country has in its wisdom contrived for me the most insignificant office that ever the invention of man contrived or his imagination conceived.

JOHN ADAMS, THE FIRST VICE PRESIDENT, DESCRIBING THE VICE PRES-
IDENCY IN A LETTER TO HIS WIFE ABIGAIL, 1793

Nearly all men can stand adversity, but if you want to test a man's character, give him power.

ABRAHAM LINCOLN

POLITICIAN, n. An eel in the fundamental mud upon which the superstructure of organized society is reared. When he wriggles he mistakes the agitation of his tail for the trembling of the edifice. As compared with the statesman, he suffers the disadvantage of being alive.

AMBROSE BIERCE, *THE DEVIL'S DICTIONARY* (1906)

Suppose you were an idiot. And suppose you were a member of Congress. But I repeat myself.

MARK TWAIN

———

You can't use tact with a Congressman! A Congressman is a hog! You must take a stick and hit him on the snout!

ANONYMOUS REMARK BY CABINET MEMBER, QUOTED BY HENRY ADAMS IN *THE EDUCATION OF HENRY ADAMS,* 1907

Is not every man sometimes a radical in politics? Men are conservatives when they are least vigorous, or when they are most luxurious. They are conservatives after dinner, or before taking their rest; when they are sick, or aged. In the morning, or when their intellect or their conscience has been aroused; when they hear music, or when they read poetry, they are radicals.

RALPH WALDO EMERSON, "NEW ENGLAND REFORMERS," 1844

Any man who is not something of a socialist before he is forty has no heart. Any man who is still a socialist after he is forty has no head.

WENDELL L. WILKIE

The more you observe politics, the more you've got to admit that each party is worse than the other.

WILL ROGERS

The Democratic Party is like a mule. It has neither pride of ancestry nor hope of posterity.

IGNATIUS DONNELLY, POLITICIAN, 1860

———

A conservative is a liberal who's been mugged.

ANONYMOUS

A liberal is a conservative who has been arrested.

Tom Wolfe, *The Bonfire of the Vanities* (1987)

A liberal is a person whose interests aren't at stake at the moment.

Willis Player

How a minority,
Reaching majority,
Seizing authority,
Hates a minority!

ATTRIBUTED TO LEONARD HARMAN ROBBINS

The two real political parties in America are the Winners and the Losers. The people don't acknowledge this. They claim membership in two imaginary parties, the Republicans and the Democrats, instead.

KURT VONNEGUT, *WAMPETERS, FOMA AND GRANFALLOONS* (1974)

Politics is the reflex of the business and industrial world.

EMMA GOLDMAN, *ANARCHISM AND OTHER ESSAYS* (1910)

·•·•·

The whole aim of practical politics is to keep the populace alarmed (and hence clamorous to be led to safety) by menacing it with an endless series of hobgoblins, all of them imaginary.

H. L. MENCKEN, "WOMAN AS OUTLAWS" IN *A MENCKEN CHRESTOMATHY* (1949)

I am deeply touched—not as deeply touched as you have been coming to this dinner, but nevertheless it is a sentimental occasion.

SENATOR JOHN F. KENNEDY, REMARKS AT A FUND-RAISING DINNER, 1960

Don't buy a single vote more than necessary. I'll be damned if I'm going to pay for a landslide.

TELEGRAPHED MESSAGE READ ALOUD BY JOHN F. KENNEDY AT A GRIDIRON DINNER IN 1958, ALLEGEDLY FROM HIS FATHER, BUT PROBABLY WRITTEN BY KENNEDY HIMSELF, QUOTED IN CUTLER, *HONEY FITZ* (1962)

An honest politician is one who when he's bought stays bought.

SIMON CAMERON, ATTRIBUTED, C. 1850

Never put anything in writing that you can convey by a wink or nod.

EARL LONG

All politics is local.

THOMAS P. "TIP" O'NEILL

Vote early and vote often.

ANONYMOUS, 1850S

It is by the goodness of God that in our country we have those three unspeakably precious things: freedom of speech, freedom of conscience, and the prudence never to practice either.

MARK TWAIN

———•••———

Practical politics consists in ignoring facts.

HENRY ADAMS

Freedom of the press is guaranteed only to those who own one.

A. J. Liebling, American journalist, quoted in Kluger, *The Paper: The Life and Death of the New York Herald Tribune* (1986)

Democracy is the theory that the common people know what they want, and deserve to get it good and hard.

H. L. Mencken, journalist and literary critic, *A Little Book in C Major* (1916)

Ma, ma, where's my Pa?

SLOGAN USED IN 1884 AGAINST PRESIDENTIAL CANDIDATE GROVER
CLEVELAND, WHO HAD FATHERED AN ILLEGITIMATE CHILD;
CLEVELAND WON THE ELECTION

A chicken in every pot, a car in every garage.

ANONYMOUS, REPUBLICAN PRESIDENTIAL CAMPAIGN SLOGAN, 1928

I didn't say that I didn't say it. I said that I didn't say that I said it. I want to make that very clear.

ATTRIBUTED TO GEORGE ROMNEY, *NATIONAL REVIEW*, DECEMBER 12, 1967

People have got to know whether or not their president is a crook. Well, I'm not a crook.

RICHARD M. NIXON, PRESS CONFERENCE, NOVEMBER 17, 1973

When the President does it, that means that it is not illegal.

RICHARD M. NIXON, TELEVISED INTERVIEW, MAY 20, 1977

I've looked on a lot of women with lust. I've committed adultery in my heart many times. This is something God recognizes I will do—and I have done it— and God forgives me for it.

JIMMY CARTER, INTERVIEW IN *PLAYBOY* DURING PRESIDENTIAL CAMPAIGN AGAINST GERALD FORD, 1976

Politics is just like show business, you have a hell of an opening, coast for a while and then have a hell of a close.

RONALD REAGAN, REMARK TO AIDE IN 1966

One word sums up probably the responsibility of any vice president, and that one word is "to be prepared."

J. DANFORTH QUAYLE

I did not have sexual relations with that woman, Miss Lewinsky.

BILL CLINTON, JANUARY 26, 1998

Politics is the best show in America.

WILL ROGERS, 1932

Against the assault of laughter nothing can stand.

MARK TWAIN, *THE MYSTERIOUS STRANGER* (1916)

American Ingenuity

The man with a new idea is a crank until the idea succeeds.

MARK TWAIN

Eripuit coelo fulmen, sceptrumque tyrannis
(He snatched the lightning shaft from heaven, and the sceptre from tyrants)

INSCRIPTION FOR A BUST OF BENJAMIN FRANKLIN

If we don't improve our product, somebody else will.

JOHN DEERE

What hath God wrought!

BIBLICAL QUOTATION USED BY SAMUEL MORSE AS THE FIRST
ELECTRIC TELEGRAPH MESSAGE, MAY 24, 1844

Our inventions are wont to be pretty toys, which distract our attention from serious things. They are but improved means to an unimproved end. We are in great haste to construct a magnetic telegraph from Maine to Texas; but Maine and Texas, it may be, have nothing important to communicate.

HENRY DAVID THOREAU, *WALDEN* (1854)

Members must strictly observe the time agreed upon for exercise, and be punctual in their attendance.

ALEXANDER J. CARTWRIGHT, WRITING THE FIRST OF THE 20 RULES HE DEVISED ON SEPTEMBER 23, 1845 TO GOVERN THE PLAY OF HIS KNICKERBOCKER BASE BALL CLUB

To invent you need a good imagination and a pile of junk.

THOMAS ALVA EDISON

There is no country in the world where machinery is so lovely as in America.

OSCAR WILDE, "PERSONAL IMPRESSIONS OF AMERICA," 1883

—•••—

Bridges are America's cathedrals.

ANONYMOUS

Ferris is a crackpot.

REMARK OF AN OFFICIAL AT THE WORLD'S COLUMBIAN EXHIBITION OF 1893 WHEN GEORGE FERRIS—A BRIDGE-BUILDER FROM PITTSBURGH—UNVEILED HIS PLANS FOR A 264-FOOT-HIGH "OBSERVATION WHEEL."

You push the button, we do the rest.

GEORGE EASTMAN, ON HIS NEW KODAK CAMERA

I date the end of the old republic and the birth of the empire to the invention, in the late thirties, of air conditioning. Before air conditioning, Washington was deserted from mid-June to September.

GORE VIDAL, "AT HOME IN WASHINGTON, D.C.," ESSAYS 1983–1987 (1987)

The virgin fertility of our soils and the vast amount of unskilled labor have been more of a curse than a blessing to agriculture.

GEORGE WASHINGTON CARVER, THE NEED OF SCIENTIFIC AGRICULTURE IN THE SOUTH (1902)

When one door closes another door opens; but we so often look so long and so regretfully upon the closed door, that we do not see the ones which open for us.

ALEXANDER GRAHAM BELL

We were lucky enough to grow up in an environment where there was always much encouragement to children to pursue intellectual interests; to investigate whatever aroused curiosity.

ORVILLE WRIGHT

I believe my ardour for invention springs from his loins. I can't say that the brassiere will ever take as great a place in history as the steamboat, but I did invent it.

CARESSE CROSBY, ON HER FORBEAR ROBERT FULTON, INVENTOR OF THE FIRST COMMERCIAL STEAMBOAT

Any color—so long as it's black.

HENRY FORD ON THE COLOR CHOICE FOR THE MODEL T FORD, 1916

The history of astronomy is a history of receding horizons.

EDWIN HUBBLE

———•❖•———

He felt he had created kind of a monster.

KENT FARNSWORTH, REFERRING TO HIS FATHER PHILO T. FARNSWORTH, THE INVENTOR OF TELEVISION

Go to jail. Go directly to jail. Do not pass go. Do not collect $200.

CHARLES BRACE DARROW, INSTRUCTIONS FOR THE GAME MONOPOLY, 1935

There is a natural hootchy-kootchy motion to a gold-fish.

WALT DISNEY, QUOTED IN *PROFILES IN AMERICA*, CROWELL (1954)

I think and think for months and years. Ninety-nine times, the conclusion is false. The hundredth time I am right.

ALBERT EINSTEIN

We turned the switch, saw the flashes, watched for ten minutes, then switched everything off and went home. That night I knew the world was headed for sorrow.

LEO SZILARD, U.S. PHYSICIST BORN IN HUNGARY, RECALLING THE 1939 EXPERIMENT THAT CONFIRMED ATOMS COULD BE SPLIT

Whatever Nature has in store for mankind, unpleasant as it may be, men must accept, for ignorance is never better than knowledge.

ENRICO FERMI

Never tell people how to do things. Tell them what to do and they will surprise you with their ingenuity.

GENERAL GEORGE S. PATTON JR.

The difficult we do immediately. The impossible takes a little longer.

U.S. ARMY SERVICE FORCES, MOTTO DURING WORLD WAR II

When you see something that is technically sweet, you go ahead and do it and you argue about what to do about it only after you have had your technical success. That is the way it was with the atomic bomb.

J. ROBERT OPPENHEIMER, PHYSICIST WHO LED THE PUSH TO DEVELOP THE ATOMIC BOMB DURING WORLD WAR II

The work of the individual still remains the spark that moves mankind ahead even more than team-work.

IGOR SIKORSKY, BEST KNOWN FOR DEVELOPING THE HELICOPTER

It's Slinky, it's Slinky, for fun it's a wonderful toy
It's Slinky, it's Slinky, it's fun for a girl and a boy

SLINKY AD JINGLE

From then on, when anything went wrong with a computer, we said it had bugs in it.

GRACE MURRAY HOPPER, ON THE REMOVAL OF A 2-INCH MOTH FROM AN EARLY COMPUTER IN 1945, QUOTED IN *TIME*, APRIL 16, 1984

At this very moment, we have the necessary techniques, both material and psychological, to create a full and satisfying life for everyone.

B. F. SKINNER, *WALDEN TWO* (1948)

When I am working on a problem, I never think about beauty, but when I have finished, if the solution is not beautiful, I know it is wrong.

R. BUCKMINSTER FULLER

The people—could you patent the sun?

JONAS E. SALK, AMERICAN VIROLOGIST, WHEN ASKED WHO OWNED THE PATENT ON HIS POLIO VACCINE, THE WORLD'S FIRST, QUOTED IN *FAMOUS MEN OF SCIENCE*, S. BOLTON

I believe that this nation should commit itself to achieving the goal, before this decade is out, of landing a man on the moon and returning him safely to the earth.

PRESIDENT JOHN F. KENNEDY, ADDRESS TO JOINT SESSION OF CONGRESS, MAY 25, 1961

Biology has at least 50 more interesting years.

JAMES D. WATSON, AMERICAN BIOLOGIST, REMARK MADE IN 1984

America is now a space-faring nation, a frontier good for millions of years. The only time remotely comparable was when Columbus discovered a whole new world.

JAMES MCDONNELL, BUILDER OF MERCURY AND GEMINI SPACE CAPSULES, *TIME*, MARCH 31, 1967

If you were plowing a field, which would you rather use? Two strong oxen or 1,024 chickens?

SEYMOUR CRAY, INVENTOR OF THE SUPERCOMPUTER

I don't try to describe the future. I try to prevent it.

RAY BRADBURY, SCIENCE FICTION AUTHOR, *INDEPENDENT*, JULY 16, 1992

Everyone who's ever taken a shower has an idea. It's the person who gets out of the shower, dries off and does something about it who makes a difference.

NOLAN BUSHNELL, INVENTOR OF EARLY VIDEO GAME PONG, 1971

You read about technological revolutions, the Industrial Revolution, and here was one happening and I was part of it.

STEVE WOZNIAK, WHO WITH STEVE JOBS INVENTED THE FIRST
READY-MADE PERSONAL COMPUTER AND CREATED APPLE

———

We live in a society exquisitely dependent on science and technology, in which hardly anyone knows anything about science and technology.

CARL SAGAN, AMERICAN ASTRONOMER

This was the last major event of atmospheric flight. That we did it as private citizens says a lot about freedom in America.

RICHARD G. RUTAN, UPON COMPLETING THE FIRST NONSTOP FLIGHT AROUND THE WORLD ON ONE TANK OF GAS IN THE EXPERIMENTAL PLANE *VOYAGER*, 1986

Houston, Tranquility Base here. The Eagle has landed.

NEIL A. ARMSTRONG, FIRST MESSAGE SENT TO EARTH AFTER THE APOLLO 11 LUNAR MODULE *EAGLE* LANDING JULY 20, 1969

To see the earth as we now see it, small and beautiful in that eternal silence where it floats, is to see ourselves as riders on the earth together, brothers on that bright loveliness in the unending night.

ARCHIBALD MACLEISH, "RIDERS ON EARTH TOGETHER, BROTHERS IN ETERNAL COLD," *THE NEW YORK TIMES*, DECEMBER 25, 1968

Money and Business

The chief business of the American people is business. They are profoundly concerned with producing, buying, selling, investing and prospering in the world.

CALVIN COOLIDGE, 1925

There is America, which at this day serves for little more than to amuse you with stories of savage men and uncouth manners, yet shall, before you taste of death, show itself equal to the whole of that commerce which now attracts the envy of the world.

EDMUND BURKE, IRISH STATESMAN, 1729–1797

God helps them that help themselves.

BENJAMIN FRANKLIN, MAXIM FROM *POOR RICHARD'S ALMANAC* (1757)

I've been nitpicked to pieces by the goddamn bureau-
cracy.

TRAVIS REED

The business of government is to keep the government out of business—that is, unless business needs
government aid.

WILL ROGERS (1879–1935)

Hardly anything but money remains to create strongly marked differences between them and to raise some of them above the common level.

ALEXIS DE TOCQUEVILLE, *DEMOCRACY IN AMERICA* (1835)

———

Banking establishments are more dangerous than standing armies.

THOMAS JEFFERSON, LETTER, 1816

In the main it will be found that a power over a man's support is a power over his will.

ALEXANDER HAMILTON, *THE FEDERALIST*, NO. 73. (BY "SUPPORT" HE MEANS SALARY.)

———

There is always room at the top.

DANIEL WEBSTER, SENATOR AND ORATOR, WHEN WARNED ABOUT THE LONG ODDS HE WOULD FACE AS A LAWYER

People of the same trade seldom meet together, even for merriment and diversion, but the conversation ends in a conspiracy against the public, or in some contrivance to raise prices.

ADAM SMITH, *WEALTH OF NATIONS* (1776)

No nation was ever ruined by trade.

BENJAMIN FRANKLIN, *THOUGHTS ON COMMERCIAL SUBJECTS*

There is no such thing as a free lunch.

ANONYMOUS

If a man can write a better book, preach a better sermon, or make a better mouse-trap, than his neighbor,
though he build his house in the woods, the world
will make a beaten path to his door.

RALPH WALDO EMERSON

All you need in this life is ignorance and confidence;
then success is sure.

MARK TWAIN, LETTER, 1887

———•·•·•———

No one in this world, so far as I know, has ever lost
money by underestimating the intelligence of the
great masses of the plain people.

H. L. MENCKEN, *CHICAGO TRIBUNE*, SEPTEMBER 19, 1926

There's a sucker born every minute.

PHINEAS T. BARNUM, SHOWMAN, ATTRIBUTED

———•••———

Never give a sucker an even break.

W. C. FIELDS, *POPPY*, A MOVIE FROM 1936

America has meant to the world a land in which the common man who means well and is willing to do his part has access to all the necessary means of a good life.

ALVIN SAUNDERS JOHNSON

In an English ship, they say, it is poor grub, poor pay, and easy work; in an American ship, good grub, good pay, and hard work. And this is applicable to the working populations of both countries.

JACK LONDON, *THE PEOPLE OF THE ABYSS*

Burn down your cities and leave our farms and your cities will spring up again as if by magic. But destroy our farms and grass will grow in the streets of every city in this country.

WILLIAM JENNINGS BRYAN, "CROSS OF GOLD SPEECH," DELIVERED AT THE DEMOCRATIC NATIONAL CONVENTION IN 1896

Never invest your money in anything that eats or needs repainting.

BILLY ROSE, IN THE NEW YORK POST

Take care to sell your horse before he dies. The art of life is passing losses on.

ROBERT FROST, "THE INGENUITIES OF DEBT"

Take away my people, but leave my factories, and soon grass will grow on the factory floors. Take away my factories, but leave my people, and soon we will have a new and better factory.

ANDREW CARNEGIE, INDUSTRIALIST AND PHILANTHROPIST

Let me tell you about the very rich. They are different from you and me.

F. SCOTT FITZGERALD, *ALL THE SAD YOUNG MEN* (1926)

Conspicuous consumption of valuable goods is a means of reputability to the gentleman of leisure.

THORSTEIN BUNDE VEBLEN, *THE THEORY OF THE LEISURE CLASS* (1899)

The growth of a large business is merely a survival of the fittest. The American beauty rose can be produced in the splendour and fragrance which bring cheer to its beholder only by sacrificing the early buds which grow up around it.

JOHN D. ROCKEFELLER, INDUSTRIALIST AND PHILANTHROPIST,
QUOTED IN *OUR BENEVOLENT FEUDALISM* (1902)

We accept and welcome as conditions to which we must accommodate ourselves, great inequality of environment; the concentration of business, industrial and commercial, in the hands of a few; and the law of competition between these, as being not only beneficial, but essential for the future progress of the race.

ANDREW CARNEGIE, 1889

The public be damned! I am working for my stock-holders.

WILLIAM HENRY VANDERBILT, RAILWAY MAGNATE

———

A business that makes nothing but money is a poor kind of business.

HENRY FORD

Monopoly is business at the end of its journey.

HENRY DEMAREST LLOYD, 1894

We demand that big business give people a square deal.

THEODORE ROOSEVELT, IN REFERENCE TO U.S. STEEL, 1901

When I want to buy up any politician I always find
the anti-monopolists the most purchasable—they
don't come so high.

WILLIAM HENRY VANDERBILT, 1882

CORPORATION, n. An ingenious device for obtaining individual profit without individual responsibility.

AMBROSE BIERCE, THE DEVIL'S DICTIONARY (1906)

The low level which commercial morality has reached in America is deplorable. We have humble God-fearing Christian men among us who will stoop to do things for a million dollars that they ought not to be willing to do for less than 2 millions.

MARK TWAIN

Under capitalism, man exploits man. Under communism, it's just the opposite.

JOHN KENNETH GALBRAITH

⸺•·•⸺

I don't think my name will mean much to the bear business, but you're welcome to use it.

THEODORE ROOSEVELT, LETTER TO THE MANUFACTURER OF THE FIRST TEDDY BEAR, 1903

The treasury of America depends upon the inventions of unknown men; upon the originations of unknown men, upon the ambitions of unknown men. Every country is renewed out of the ranks of the unknown, not out of the ranks of those already famous and powerful and in control.

WOODROW WILSON, *THE NEW FREEDOM* (1913)

No man's credit is as good as his money.

ED HOWE

I have found out in later years we were very poor, but the glory of America is that we didn't know it then.

DWIGHT D. EISENHOWER

We grew up founding our dreams on the infinite promise of American advertising.

ZELDA FITZGERALD, *SAVE ME THE WALTZ* (1932)

Let me remind you that credit is the lifeblood of business, the lifeblood of prices and jobs.

PRESIDENT HERBERT HOOVER, SPEECH, 1932

If Americans are going to start worrying about whether they can afford a thing or not, you are going to ruin the whole characteristic of our people.

WILL ROGERS

All the American women had purple noses and gray lips and their faces were chalk white from terrible powder. I recognized that the United States could be my life's work.

HELENA RUBINSTEIN, COSMETICS EXECUTIVE, RECALLING HER ARRIVAL IN AMERICA IN 1914

Freedom is the oxygen without which science cannot breathe.

DAVID SARNOFF, CHAIRMAN, RCA

———

This is virgin territory for whorehouses.

AL CAPONE, REFERRING TO SUBURBAN CHICAGO

The country needs and, unless I mistake its temper, the country demands bold, persistent experimentation. It is common sense to take a method and try it. If it fails, admit it frankly and try another.

Franklin D. Roosevelt, 1932

It's a recession when your neighbor loses his job; it's a depression when you lose your own.

Harry S Truman

There is no security on this earth; there is only opportunity.

DOUGLAS MACARTHUR

I learned that good judgment comes from experience and that experience grows out of mistakes.

GENERAL OMAR N. BRADLEY, U.S. ARMY

For years I thought what was good for our country was good for General Motors and vice versa. The difference did not exist.

CHARLES WILSON, HEAD OF GENERAL MOTORS CORPORATION, DURING HEARINGS ON HIS NOMINATION AS SECRETARY OF DEFENSE, JANUARY 15, 1953

A certain kind of rich man afflicted with the symptoms of moral dandyism sooner or later comes to the conclusion that it isn't enough merely to make money. He feels obliged to hold views, to espouse causes and elect Presidents. The spectacle is nearly always comic.

LEWIS H. LAPHAM, *MONEY AND CLASS IN AMERICA* (1988)

We must open the doors of opportunity. But we must also equip our people to walk through those doors.

LYNDON BAINES JOHNSON

———•••••———

I never wanted to be a crumb. If I had to be a crumb, I'd rather be dead.

SALVATORE "LUCKY" LUCIANO

Owning your own home is America's unique recipe for avoiding revolution and promoting pseudo-equality at the same time. To keep citizens puttering in their yards instead of sputtering on the barricades, the government has gladly deprived itself of billions in tax revenues.

FLORENCE KING, "DEMOCRACY," *REFLECTIONS IN A JAUNDICED EYE* (1989)

What's great about this country is that America started the tradition where the richest consumers buy essentially the same things as the poorest.

ANDY WARHOL, *FROM A TO B AND BACK AGAIN* (1975)

———•••———

Doing well that which should not be done at all.

GORE VIDAL, OFFERING A DEFINITION OF COMMERCIALISM

Government's view of the economy could be summed up in a few short phrases: If it moves, tax it. If it keeps moving, regulate it. And if it stops moving, subsidize it.

RONALD REAGAN

Only the little people pay taxes.

LEONA HELMSLEY, HOTEL MAGNATE, AS QUOTED IN *NEWSWEEK*, JULY 24, 1989

It is our job to make women unhappy with what they have.

B. EARL PUCKETT, PRESIDENT, ALLIED STORES CORPORATION

Touch a face. Touch a hand. Say, "This is for you, this is what I want you to wear."

ESTÉE LAUDER, COSMETICS EXECUTIVE, INSTRUCTING HER SALES FORCE, QUOTED BY KENNEDY FRASER IN *THE NEW YORKER*, SEPTEMBER 15, 1986

It is capitalist America that produced the modern independent woman. Never in history have women had more freedom of choice in regard to dress, behavior, career, and sexual orientation.

CAMILLE PAGLIA, IN *SEX, ART, AND AMERICAN CULTURE* (1992)

Americans want action for their money. They are fascinated by its self-reproducing qualities if it's put to work. Gold-hoarding goes against the American grain; it fits in better with European pessimism than with America's traditional optimism.

PAULA NELSON, BUSINESS EXECUTIVE, *THE JOY OF MONEY* (1975)

To turn $100 into $110 is work. To turn $100 million into $110 million is inevitable.

EDGAR BRONFMAN, CHAIRMAN OF SEAGRAM COMPANY, 1985

Greed is healthy.

IVAN F. BOESKY, 1986

Be nice to people on your way up because you'll meet
them on your way down.

WILSON MIZNER

———•—•••—•———

The secret point of money and power in America is
neither the things that money can buy nor power for
power's sake, but absolute personal freedom, mobility, privacy. It is the instinct which drove America to
the Pacific.

JOAN DIDION, *SLOUCHING TOWARDS BETHLEHEM* (1967)

The meek shall inherit the earth, but not the mineral rights.

J. PAUL GETTY

—•••—

You can get more with a nice word and a gun than you can with a nice word.

AL CAPONE

War

To be prepared for war is one of the most effectual means of preserving peace.

GEORGE WASHINGTON, SPEECH TO CONGRESS, JANUARY 8, 1790

There never was a good war or a bad peace.

BENJAMIN FRANKLIN, LETTER, JULY 27, 1783

To delight in war is a merit in the soldier, a dangerous quality in the captain, and a positive crime in the
statesman.

GEORGE SANTAYANA, PHILOSOPHER, *THE LIFE OF REASON*
(1905–1906)

———

I heard the bullets whistle, and believe me, there is
something charming in the sound.

GEORGE WASHINGTON, RECALLING A SKIRMISH IN THE FRENCH AND
INDIAN WAR (1754)

I have not yet begun to fight.

JOHN PAUL JONES, WHEN ASKED IF HE WAS READY TO SURRENDER TO
THE BRITISH FRIGATE *SERAPIS*, SEPTEMBER 23, 1779

In the present civil war it is quite possible that God's
purpose is something different from the purpose of
either party.

ABRAHAM LINCOLN, SEPTEMBER 2, 1862, *COLLECTED WORKS OF*
ABRAHAM LINCOLN (1953)

If you don't want to use the army, I should like to borrow it for a while. Yours respectfully, A. Lincoln.

ABRAHAM LINCOLN, ADMONISHING GEN. GEORGE B. MCCLELLAN
FOR HIS LACK OF AGGRESSION

The art of war is simple enough. Find out where your enemy is. Get at him as soon as you can. Strike at him as hard as you can and as often as you can, and keep moving on.

ULYSSES S. GRANT, ATTRIBUTED

It is well that war is so terrible: we would grow too fond of it!

ROBERT E. LEE, CONFEDERATE GENERAL, DURING THE BATTLE OF FREDERICKSBURG, DECEMBER 13, 1862

War is cruelty, and you cannot refine it.

GENERAL WILLIAM T. SHERMAN, LETTER, SEPTEMBER 12, 1864

My country is bleeding, my people are perishing around me. But I feel as a South Carolinian, I am bound to tell the North, go on! go on!

ANGELINA GRIMKÉ, ABOLITIONIST, SPEECH ON MAY 14, 1863

The real war will never get in the books. And so goodbye to the war.

WALT WHITMAN, "THE REAL WAR WILL NEVER GET IN THE BOOKS," 1882

War is a blessing compared with national degradation.

ANDREW JACKSON, LETTER, MAY 2, 1845

Hear me. I am tired. My heart is sick and sad. Our chiefs are dead; the little children are freezing. My people have no blankets, no food. From where the sun stands, I will fight no more forever.

CHIEF JOSEPH THE YOUNGER, SPOKEN AT THE END OF THE NEZ PERCÉ WAR, 1877

Don't hit at all if it is honorably possible to avoid hitting; but never hit soft.

THEODORE ROOSEVELT

From the Halls of Montezuma,
To the shores of Tripoli,
We fight our country's battles,
On the land as on the sea.

"THE MARINE'S HYMN," 1847

Don't cheer, men; those poor devils are dying.

JOHN WOODWARD PHILIP, COMMANDER OF THE TEXAS DURING THE
SPANISH-AMERICAN WAR, RESTRAINING HIS CREW DURING THE
NAVAL BATTLE OFF SANTIAGO, WHERE THE SPANISH FLEET WAS DECI-
MATED, 1898

There are two things which will always be very difficult for a democratic nation: to start a war and to end
it.

ALEXIS DE TOCQUEVILLE, FRENCH PHILOSOPHER, *DEMOCRACY IN
AMERICA* (1835)

The American people is out to get the kaiser. Anybody who gets in the way of the great machine the energy and devotion of a hundred million patriots is building towards the stainless purpose of saving civilization from the Huns will be mashed like a fly. Don't monkey with the buzzsaw.

JOHN DOS PASSOS, FROM THE NOVEL *U.S.A.* (1937)

Come on, you sons of bitches! Do you want to live forever?

DANIEL DALY, U.S. MARINE, SPOKEN AT BATTLE OF BELLEAU WOOD, JUNE 4, 1918

The most serious thing about war is the slaughter of boys. It is the boys of the country who must face the enemy.

REBECCA LATIMER FELTON, *COUNTRY LIFE IN GEORGIA IN THE DAYS OF MY YOUTH* (1919)

France was a land, England was a people, but America, having about it still that quality of the idea, was harder to utter—it was the graves at Shiloh and the tired, drawn, nervous faces of its great men, and the country boys dying in the Argonne for a phrase that was empty before their bodies withered. It was a willingness of the heart.

F. SCOTT FITZGERALD, "THE SWIMMERS," *SATURDAY EVENING POST,* OCTOBER 19, 1929

All of you young people who served in the war. You are a lost generation. You have no respect for anything. You drink yourselves to death.

GERTRUDE STEIN, REMARK TO ERNEST HEMINGWAY REFERRING TO VETERANS OF WWI

———

Drilling and arming, when carried on on a national scale, excite whole populations to frenzies which end in war.

FRANKLIN D. ROOSEVELT, LETTER TO THE PRIME MINISTER OF GREAT BRITAIN, 1933

If it moves, salute it. If it doesn't move, pick it up. If you can't pick it up, paint it.

NAVY SAYING

And while I am talking to you mothers and fathers, I give you one more assurance. I have said this before, but I shall say it again and again and again: Your boys are not going to be sent into any foreign wars.

FRANKLIN D. ROOSEVELT, OCTOBER 30, 1940

Praise the Lord and pass the ammunition.

HOWELL FORGY, NAVAL CHAPLAIN, SAID WHILE HANDING OUT
AMMUNITION DURING THE ATTACK ON PEARL HARBOR, DECEMBER 7,
1941

Our job is now clear. All Americans must be prepared
to make, on a 24-hour schedule, every war weapon
possible and the war factory line will use men and
materials which will bring the war effort to every
man, woman, and child in America.

LYNDON BAINES JOHNSON, DECEMBER 8, 1941

This world crisis came about without women having anything to do with it. If the women of the world had not been excluded from world affairs, things today might have been different.

ALICE PAUL, SPEAKING IN 1941, QUOTED IN *MOVERS AND SHAKERS* (1973)

Gentleman, we are being killed on the beaches. Let's go inland and be killed.

GENERAL NORMAN COTA, ON OMAHA BEACH, FRANCE, ON D-DAY, JUNE 6, 1944

There were wrecks everywhere—wrecks of vehicles everywhere, wrecks of men everywhere.

CHARLES EARLY, WORLD WAR II VETERAN, RECALLING THE BATTLE OF IWO JIMA, *THE NEW YORK TIMES*, FEBRUARY 20, 1985

In war, you win or lose, live or die—and the difference is just an eyelash.

GENERAL DOUGLAS MACARTHUR

There are no atheists in foxholes.

WILLIAM THOMAS CUMMINGS, AMERICAN PRIEST, SERMON IN
BATAAN, 1942

When I began to use my cricket, the first man I met
in the darkness I thought was a German until he
cricketed. . . . We threw our arms around each other,
and from that moment I knew we had won the war.

GENERAL MAXWELL D. TAYLOR, REMEMBERING D-DAY, QUOTED IN
TIME, MAY 28, 1984

They may walk with a little less spring in their step, and the ranks are growing thinner, but let us never forget, when they were young, these men saved the world.

BILL CLINTON, SPEECH IN NORMANDY ON JUNE 6, 1994, THE FIFTIETH ANNIVERSARY OF THE ALLIED LANDING

The American cemetery at Saint-Laurent-sur-Mer is a great lawn at the edge of the sea, white marble crosses and Stars of David against an open horizon, very American in the best sense: no phony piety, simple, easy.

JOHN VINOCUR, "D-DAY PLUS 40 YEARS," THE NEW YORK TIMES, MAY 13, 1984

Orr would be crazy to fly more missions and sane if he didn't, but if he was sane he had to fly them. If he flew them he was crazy and didn't have to; but if he didn't want to he was sane and had to.

JOSEPH HELLER, *CATCH-22* (1961)

I hate war as only a soldier who has lived it can, only as one who has seen its brutality, its stupidity.

DWIGHT D. EISENHOWER, JANUARY 10, 1946

I am become death, the shatterer of worlds.

ROBERT J. OPPENHEIMER, QUOTING FROM THE *GITA* AT THE FIRST
ATOMIC TEST, JULY 16, 1945

Either war is obsolete or men are.

R. BUCKMINSTER FULLER, *THE NEW YORKER*, 1966

The object of war is not to die for your country but to make the other bastard die for his.

GENERAL GEORGE S. PATTON JR.

———

Gentlemen, we're not retreating. We are just advancing in a different direction.

GENERAL OLIVER P. SMITH, RETREATING BEFORE A VASTLY LARGER CHINESE FORCE DURING THE KOREAN WAR, DECEMBER 4, 1950

Nothing so comforts the military mind as the maxim of a great but dead general.

BARBARA TUCHMAN, *THE GUNS OF AUGUST* (1962)

I didn't fire him because he was a dumb son of a bitch, although he was, but that's not against the law for generals. If it was, half to three-quarters of them would be in jail.

HARRY S TRUMAN, ON GENERAL MACARTHUR

We must guard against the acquisition of unwarranted influence, whether sought or unsought, by the military-industrial complex. The potential for the disastrous rise of misplaced power exists and will persist.

DWIGHT D. EISENHOWER, FAREWELL ADDRESS, JANUARY 17, 1961

Kennedy said that if we had nuclear war we'd kill 300 million people in the first hour. McNamara, who is a good businessman and likes to save, says it would be only 200 million.

NORMAN THOMAS, RECALLED ON HIS DEATH IN 1968

Gentlemen! You can't fight in here! This is the war room!

FROM *DR. STRANGELOVE OR: HOW I LEARNED TO STOP WORRYING AND LOVE THE BOMB*, DIRECTED BY STANLEY KUBRICK, 1964

All of us who grew up before the war are immigrants in time, immigrants from an earlier world. The young are at home here. Their eyes have always seen satellites in the sky. They have never known a world in which war did not mean annihilation.

MARGARET MEAD, *CULTURE AND COMMITMENT* (1970)

I told them I'm not going to let Vietnam go the way of China. I told them to go back and tell those generals in Saigon that I want something for my money. I want 'em to get off their butts and get out in those jungles and whip hell out of some Communists.

LYNDON BAINES JOHNSON, QUOTED IN *NEWSWEEK*, FEBRUARY 10, 1975

War is the unfolding of miscalculations.

BARBARA TUCHMAN, *THE GUNS OF AUGUST* (1962)

And in that time
When men decide and feel safe
To call the war insane,
Take one moment to embrace
Those gentle heroes
You left behind.

MAJOR MICHAEL DAVIS O'DONNELL, U.S. ARMY, FROM A POEM
WRITTEN IN 1970, THREE MONTHS BEFORE HIS DEATH IN VIETNAM

Exactly who the men on the hill are is not as important as the fact that they are there. Being there, they are not only representative of other men who died unknown, but of all men who have fought for America. For that reason, they belong to all of us.

JOHN C. METZLER, SUPERINTENDENT, ARLINGTON NATIONAL CEMETERY, 1958

Our strategy in going after this army is very simple. First we are going to cut it off, and then we are going to kill it.

GENERAL COLIN POWELL, DESCRIBING THE UNITED STATES' STRATEGY AGAINST IRAQ, JANUARY 23, 1991

Since September 11, an entire generation of young Americans has gained new understanding of the value of freedom and its cost and duty and its sacrifice. The battle is now joined on many fronts.

PRESIDENT GEORGE W. BUSH, ANNOUNCING MILITARY STRIKES AGAINST AL-QA'EDA AND THE TALIBAN REGIME IN AFGHANISTAN, OCTOBER 7, 2001

America's Place in the World

We shall be a city upon a hill, the eyes of all people are on us.

JOHN WINTHROP, EARLY AMERICAN SETTLER, FROM "CHRISTIAN CHARITY, A MODEL HEREOF," A SERMON DELIVERED ON BOARD THE SHIP *ARBELLA*, 1630

I always consider the settlement of America with reverence and wonder, as the opening of a grand scene and design in providence, for the illumination of the ignorant and the emancipation of the slavish part of mankind all over the earth.

JOHN ADAMS, 1765

America is more wild and absurd than ever

EDMUND BURKE, IRISH STATESMAN, LETTER, 1769

You cannot conquer America.

WILLIAM PITT, FORMER BRITISH PRIME MINISTER, 1777

People nowadays have such high hopes of America and the political conditions obtaining there that one might say the desires, at least the secret desires, of all enlightened Europeans are deflected to the west, like our magnetic needles.

GEORG CHRISTOPH LICHTENBERG, GERMAN SCIENTIST

'Tis our true policy to steer clear of permanent alliances with any portion of the foreign world.

GEORGE WASHINGTON, FAREWELL ADDRESS, 1796

Our country! In her intercourse with foreign nations, may she always be in the right; but our country, right or wrong.

STEPHEN DECATUR, AMERICAN NAVAL COMMANDER, 1816

We owe it, therefore, to candor and to the amicable relations existing between the United States and those powers [of Europe] to declare that we should consider any attempt on their part to extend their system to any portion of this hemisphere as dangerous to our peace and safety.

JAMES MONROE, 1823

We are apt to think it the finest era of the world when America was beginning to be discovered, when a bold sailor, even if he were wrecked, might alight on a new kingdom.

GEORGE ELIOT (MARY ANN EVANS), BRITISH NOVELIST, *MIDDLEMARCH* (1871–1872)

The most important American addition to the World Experience was the simple surprising fact of America. We have helped prepare mankind for all its later surprises.

DANIEL J. BOORSTIN, HISTORIAN, "THE EXPLORING SPIRIT: AMERICA AND THE WORLD EXPERIENCE," 1975

We Americans are the peculiar, chosen people—the Israel of our time; we bear the ark of the liberties of the world.

HERMAN MELVILLE, *WHITE-JACKET* (1850)

Poor Mexico, so far from God and so close to the United States.

ATTRIBUTED PORFIRIO DIAZ, PRESIDENT OF MEXICO, 1877–1880

All the territorial possessions of all the political establishments in the earth—including America, of course—consist of pilferings from other people's wash.

MARK TWAIN, *FOLLOWING THE EQUATOR* (1897)

There is a homely adage which runs "Speak softly and carry a big stick, you will go far".

THEODORE ROOSEVELT, 1901

Every time Europe looks across the Atlantic to see the American Eagle, it observes only the rear end of an ostrich.

H. G. WELLS, ENGLISH AUTHOR

There is nothing the matter with Americans except their ideals. The real American is all right.

GILBERT KEITH CHESTERTON, BRITISH AUTHOR, 1931

Of one thing I can assure you with comparative certainty, whoever wins, Europe will be economically ruined. This war is America's great opportunity.

JOHN DOS PASSOS, FROM HIS NOVEL *U.S.A.* (1937)

In the field of world policy I would dedicate this Nation to the policy of the Good Neighbor—the neighbor who resolutely respects himself and, because he does, respects the rights of others.

FRANKLIN D. ROOSEVELT, MESSAGE TO CONGRESS, 1933

He may be a son of a bitch, but he's our son of a bitch.

FRANKLIN D. ROOSEVELT, REFERRING TO NICARAGUAN DICTATOR
ANASTASIO SOMOZA, ATTRIBUTED

Intellectually I know America is no better than any other country; emotionally I know she is better than every other country.

SINCLAIR LEWIS, 1930

The United States is like a gigantic boiler. Once the fire is lighted under it there is no limit to the power it can generate.

LORD GREY, BRITISH STATESMAN, QUOTED IN *THEIR FINEST HOUR* BY WINSTON S. CHURCHILL

Our policy is directed not against any country or doc-
trine, but against hunger, poverty, desperation, and
chaos. Its purpose should be the revival of a working
economy in the world so as to permit the emergence
of political and social conditions in which free institutions can exist.

GENERAL GEORGE MARSHALL, 1947

A police action.

PRESIDENT HARRY S TRUMAN, CHARACTERIZING U.S. INVOLVEMENT
IN KOREA, JUNE 29, 1950

———◆◆◆———

This organization is created to prevent you from
going to hell. It isn't created to take you to heaven.

HENRY CABOT LODGE JR., UNITED STATES, ON THE PURPOSE OF THE
UNITED NATIONS, 1954

Diplomacy has rarely been able to gain at the conference table what cannot be gained or held on the battlefield.

GENERAL WALTER BEDELL SMITH, 1954

The first requirement of a statesman is that he be dull. This is not always easy to achieve.

DEAN ACHESON, FORMER SECRETARY OF STATE, 1970

As you begin your tour of the United States, you may as well know that one American national trait which irritates many Americans and must be convenient for our critics is that we relentlessly advertise our imperfections.

HENRY CABOT LODGE JR., REMARK TO SOVIET PREMIER NIKITA S. KHRUSHCHEV, 1959

Whatever America hopes to bring to pass in this world must first come to pass in the heart of America.

DWIGHT D. EISENHOWER, INAUGURAL ADDRESS, 1953

America makes prodigious mistakes, America has colossal faults, but one thing cannot be denied: America is always on the move. She may be going to Hell, of course, but at least she isn't standing still.

E. E. CUMMINGS, *WHY I LIKE AMERICA* (1927)

America is a large, friendly dog in a very small room.
Every time it wags its tail it knocks over a chair.

ARNOLD TOYNBEE, BRITISH HISTORIAN, 1954

God bless the USA, so large,
So friendly, and so rich.

W. H. AUDEN, "ON THE CIRCUIT"

To those peoples in the huts and villages across the globe struggling to break the bonds of mass misery, we pledge our best efforts to help them help themselves, for whatever period is required—not because the Communists may be doing it, not because we seek their votes, but because it is right.

JOHN F. KENNEDY, INAUGURAL ADDRESS, 1961

We were eyeball-to-eyeball and the other fellow just blinked.

Dean Rusk, U.S. Secretary of State, describing the Cuban Missile Crisis, 1962

———

Vietnam presumably taught us that the United States could not serve as the world's policeman; it should also have taught us the dangers of trying to be the world's midwife to democracy when the birth is scheduled to take place under conditions of guerrilla war.

Jeane Kirkpatrick, U.S. representative at the United Nations, "Dictatorship and Double Standards," Commentary, 1979

I'm sure that President Johnson would never have pursued the war in Vietnam if he'd ever had a Fulbright to Japan, or say Bangkok, or had any feeling for what these people are like and why they acted the way they did.

J. WILLIAM FULBRIGHT, U.S. SENATOR, 1986

America is the world's living myth. There's no sense of wrong when you kill an American or blame America for some local disaster. This is our function, to be character types, to embody recurring themes that people can use to comfort themselves.

DON DELILLO, *THE NAMES* (1982)

If Kuwait grew carrots we wouldn't give a damn.

LAWRENCE KORB, FORMER ASSISTANT DEFENSE SECRETARY, REFERRING TO "OPERATION DESERT STORM," 1990

The United States is not just an old cow that gives more milk the more it's kicked in the flanks.

DEAN RUSK, U.S. SECRETARY OF STATE, 1967

———•·•·•———

The best way to enhance freedom in other lands is to demonstrate here that our democratic system is worthy of emulation.

JIMMY CARTER, 1977

Our policy is simple: We are not going to betray our friends, reward the enemies of freedom, or permit fear and retreat to become American policies, especially in this hemisphere. None of the four wars in my lifetime came about because we were too strong.

RONALD REAGAN, 1984

God and the politicians willing, the United States can declare peace upon the world, and win it.

ELY CULBERTSON, *MUST WE FIGHT RUSSIA* (1946)

Our country right or wrong! When right, to be kept right; when wrong, to be put right.

CARL SCHURZ, GERMAN-BORN U.S. SENATOR, 1872

The Arts in America

The less America looks abroad, the grander its promise.

RALPH WALDO EMERSON

No author, without a trial, can conceive of the difficulty of writing a romance about a country where there is no shadow, no antiquity, no mystery, no picturesque and gloomy wrong, nor anything but a commonplace prosperity, in broad and simple daylight, as is happily the case with my dear native land.

NATHANIEL HAWTHORNE, AUTHOR OF *THE SCARLET LETTER*, IN HIS PREFACE TO *THE MARBLE FAUN* (1860)

I celebrate myself, and sing myself.

WALT WHITMAN, "SONG OF MYSELF," 1855

———•◦•———

Oh, I never look under the hood.

E. B. WHITE, WHEN ASKED ABOUT HIS SOURCES OF INSPIRATION, 1979

So you're the little woman who wrote the book that made this great war.

ABRAHAM LINCOLN, SAID UPON MEETING HARRIET BEECHER STOWE, THE AUTHOR OF *UNCLE TOM'S CABIN*

———

I did not write it. God wrote it. I merely did his dictation.

HARRIET BEECHER STOWE, SPEAKING OF *UNCLE TOM'S CABIN* (1852)

I have found that anything that comes out of the South is going to be called grotesque by the Northern reader, unless it is grotesque, in which case it is going to be called realistic.

FLANNERY O'CONNOR, LECTURE, "SOME ASPECTS OF THE GROTESQUE IN SOUTHERN FICTION," 1960

All modern American literature comes from one book by Mark Twain called *Huckleberry Finn*.

ERNEST HEMINGWAY, *GREEN HILLS OF AFRICA* (1935)

———◦•◦———

Persons attempting to find a motive in this narrative will be prosecuted; persons attempting to find a moral in it will be banished; persons attempting to find a plot in it will be shot.

MARK TWAIN, "NOTICE—BY ORDER OF THE AUTHOR," *HUCKLEBERRY FINN* (1884)

All good writing is swimming under water and holding your breath.

F. SCOTT FITZGERALD

The most essential gift for a good writer is a built-in, shockproof, shit detector. This is the writer's radar and all great writers have had it.

ERNEST HEMINGWAY, INTERVIEW, 1958

He has never been known to use a word that might send the reader to the dictionary.

WILLIAM FAULKNER, REFERRING TO ERNEST HEMINGWAY

———•••———

Poor Faulkner. Does he really think big emotions come from big words?

ERNEST HEMINGWAY, IN RESPONSE

Books are good enough in their own way, but they are a mighty bloodless substitute for life.

ROBERT LEWIS STEVENSON, "AN APOLOGY FOR IDLERS," *VIRGINIBUS PUERISQUE* (1881)

———

The only people for me are the mad ones, the ones who are mad to live, mad to talk, mad to be saved, desirous of everything at the same time, the ones who never yawn or say a commonplace thing, but burn, burn, burn.

JACK KEROUAC, *ON THE ROAD* (1957)

I am an invisible man. I am a man of substance, of flesh and bone, fiber and liquids—and I might even be said to possess a mind. I am invisible, understand, simply because people refuse to see me.

RALPH ELLISON, OPENING PASSAGE OF *THE INVISIBLE MAN* (1952)

You cannot write for children. They're much too complicated. You can only write books that are of interest to them.

MAURICE SENDAK, 1987

In America, the race goes to the loud, the solemn, the hustler. If you think you're a great writer, you must say that you are.

GORE VIDAL, 1981

Some people say that I must be a horrible person, but that's not true. I have the heart of a young boy—in a jar on my desk.

STEPHEN KING

If I were to live my life over again, I would be an American. I would steep myself in America, I would know no other land.

HENRY JAMES, 1899

I'll die propped up in bed trying to do a poem about America.

CARL SANDBURG, HIS PLANS FOR HIS 79TH BIRTHDAY, 1957

Listen! There never was an artistic period. There never was an Art-loving nation.

JAMES McNEILL WHISTLER, AMERICAN PAINTER, 1885

Mrs. Ballinger is one of the ladies who pursue Culture in bands, as though it were dangerous to meet it alone.

EDITH WHARTON, "XINGU," *XINGU AND OTHER STORIES* (1916)

Talent! What they call talent is nothing but the capacity for doing continuous work in the right way.

WINSLOW HOMER

Every time I paint a portrait I lose a friend.

JOHN SINGER SARGENT

I said to myself—I'll paint what I see—what the flower is to me but I will paint it big and they will be surprised into taking time to look at it—I will make even busy New Yorkers take time to see what I see of flowers.

GEORGIA O'KEEFFE, 1939

When I say artist I don't mean in the narrow sense of the word—but the man who is building things—creating molding the earth. It's all a big game of construction—some with a brush—some with a shovel.

JACKSON POLLOCK, LETTER TO HIS FATHER, 1932

To me, a painter, if not the most useful, is the least harmful member of our society.

MAN RAY, AMERICAN PHOTOGRAPHER, *SELF PORTRAIT* (1963)

I unconsciously decided that, even if it wasn't an ideal world, it should be and so painted only the ideal aspects of it—pictures in which there are no drunken slatterns or self-centered mothers, only foxy grand-pas who played baseball with the kids and boys who fished from logs.

NORMAN ROCKWELL, *WASHINGTON POST,* MAY 27, 1972

Sometimes I lie awake at night and ask "Why me?"
Then a voice answers "Nothing personal, your name
just happened to come up."

CHARLIE BROWN (CREATED BY CHARLES SCHULZ)

———

The Solomon R. Guggenheim Museum is a war
between architecture and painting in which both
come out badly maimed.

JOHN CANADAY, *THE NEW YORK TIMES*, OCTOBER 21, 1959

The physician can bury his mistakes, but the architect can only advise his client to plant vines—so they should go as far as possible from home to build their first buildings.

FRANK LLOYD WRIGHT, AMERICAN ARCHITECT, *THE NEW YORK TIMES*, OCTOBER 4, 1953

I saw the Vietnam Veterans Memorial not as an object placed into the earth but as a cut in the earth that has then been polished, like a geode.

MAYA LIN, ARCHITECT OF THE MEMORIAL, *SMITHSONIAN* MAGAZINE, AUGUST 1996

I don't want it torn down. I think it's the greatest
monstrosity in America.

HARRY S TRUMAN, REFERRING TO THE OLD EXECUTIVE OFFICE
BUILDING ADJOINING THE WHITE HOUSE, 1958

———

The popular song is America's greatest ambassador.

SAMMY CAHN, 1984

It Don't Mean a Thing If It Ain't Got That Swing

DUKE ELLINGTON, SONG TITLE, 1932

I can't stand to sing the same song the same way two nights in succession, let alone two years or ten years. If you can, then it ain't music.

BILLIE HOLIDAY, *LADY SINGS THE BLUES* (1956)

We all do 'do, re, mi,' but you have got to find the other notes yourself.

LOUIS ARMSTRONG, ON JAZZ, 1956

I could depend a lot on my shaking, though I never shimmied vulgarly and only to express myself.

ETHEL WATERS, *HIS EYE IS ON THE SPARROW* (1951)

Roll over, Beethoven,
And tell Tchaikovsky the news.

CHUCK BERRY, "ROLL OVER, BEETHOVEN," 1956

The thing that influenced me most was the way
Tommy [Dorsey] played his trombone. It was my
idea to make my voice work in the same way as a
trombone or violin—not sounding like them, but
"playing" the voice like those instrumentalists.

FRANK SINATRA, QUOTED BY NANCY SINATRA, *FRANK SINATRA, MY
FATHER* (1985)

Blues is easy to play, but hard to feel.

JIMI HENDRIX, QUOTED IN MURRAY, *CROSSTOWN TRAFFIC* (1989)

It is better to make a piece of music than to perform one, better to perform one than to listen to one, better to listen to one than to misuse it as a means of distraction.

JOHN CAGE, "FORERUNNERS OF MODERN MUSIC; AT RANDOM," 1949

Singing is a trick to get people to listen to music for longer than they would ordinarily.

DAVID BYRNE, LINER NOTES TO "STOP MAKING SENSE," 1984

Music was my way of keeping people from looking through and around me. I wanted the heavies to know I was around.

BRUCE SPRINGSTEEN, 1975

When I first heard Elvis's voice I just knew that I wasn't going to work for anybody and nobody was gonna be my boss. Hearing him for the first time was like busting out of jail.

BOB DYLAN, QUOTED IN *US*, AUGUST 1987

Can't act. Can't sing. Can dance a little.

ANONYMOUS, ON FRED ASTAIRE'S FIRST SCREEN TEST

No dancer can watch Fred Astaire and not know that
we all should have been in another business.

MIKHAIL BARYSHNIKOV, RUSSIAN-AMERICAN DANCER WHO DEFECT-
ED TO THE UNITED STATES IN 1974

The real American type can never be a ballet dancer.
The legs are too long, the body too supple and the
spirit too free for this school of affected grace and toe
walking.

ISADORA DUNCAN, AMERICAN DANCER, *MY LIFE* (1927)

Theater people are always pining and agonizing because they're afraid that they'll be forgotten. And in America they're quite right. They will be.

AGNES DE MILLE, DANCER AND CHOREOGRAPHER, 1963

I think I've stretched a talent—which is so thick that it's almost opaque—over a quite unbelievable term of years.

BING CROSBY, 1956

Wave after wave of love flooded the stage and washed over me, the beginning of the one great durable romance of my life.

BETTE DAVIS, RECALLING HER FIRST SOLO CURTAIN CALL, 1977

Every country gets the circus it deserves. Spain gets bullfights. Italy gets the Catholic Church. America gets Hollywood.

ERICA JONG, "TAKE THE RED-EYE," *HOW TO SAVE YOUR OWN LIFE* (1977)

Strangely enough, the one universal myth of America—Show Business—flowered in a desert where a bunch of barely educated immigrants hoped to find the right conditions for shooting cheap movies.

FREDERIC RAPHAEL, "A WRITER STALKS THE HOLLYWOOD MYTH," *THE NEW YORK TIMES*, JANUARY 6, 1985

I was born at the age of twelve on a Metro-Goldwyn-Mayer lot.

JUDY GARLAND

We have our factory, which is called a stage. We make a product, we color it, we title it and we ship it out in cans.

CARY GRANT, 1969

It's the movies that have really been running things in America ever since they were invented. They show you what to do, how to do it, when to do it, how to feel about it, and how to look how you feel about it.

ANDY WARHOL, QUOTED IN VICTOR BOKRIS, "THE EDUCATION OF ANDY WARHOL 1937–45"

You're not a star until they can spell your name in Karachi.

HUMPHREY BOGART

Hollywood's a place where they'll pay you a thousand dollars for a kiss, and fifty cents for your soul. I know, because I turned down the first offer often enough and held out for the fifty cents.

MARILYN MONROE, IN *MARILYN MONROE IN HER OWN WORDS* (1990)

I always did like a man in uniform. And that one fits you grand. Why don't you come up sometime and see me?

MAE WEST, ACTRESS AND SEX SYMBOL, *SHE DONE HIM WRONG*, 1933

Girls bored me—they still do. I love Mickey Mouse more than any woman I've ever known.

WALT DISNEY

Ladies and gentlemen, I have a grave announcement to make. Incredible as it may seem, strange beings who landed in New Jersey tonight are the vanguard of an invading army from Mars.

ORSON WELLES, FILMMAKER, IN A RADIO MESSAGE BROADCAST AS A JOKE ON HALLOWEEN, 1938. MANY TOOK THE MESSAGE SERIOUSLY AND PANICKED.

Once a month the sky falls on my head, I come to, and I see another movie I want to make.

STEVEN SPIELBERG

———•◦•———

How could we possibly appreciate the Mona Lisa if Leonardo had written at the bottom of the canvas: "The lady is smiling because she is hiding a secret from her lover."

STANLEY KUBRICK

If my film makes one more person miserable, I've done my job.

WOODY ALLEN

An actor's a guy who, if you ain't talking about him, ain't listening.

MARLON BRANDO, 1974

Speak low and speak slow.

JOHN WAYNE, ADVICE TO YOUNG ACTORS

Who the hell wants to hear actors talk?

H. M. WARNER, FOUNDER OF WARNER BROTHERS, 1927

The happy ending is our national belief.

MARY MCCARTHY, "AMERICA THE BEAUTIFUL: THE HUMANIST IN THE BATHTUB," 1947

The Sporting Life

Americans are achievers. They are obsessed with records of achievement in sports and they keep business achievement charts on their office walls and sports awards displayed in their homes.

UNITED STATES INFORMATION AGENCY, BOOKLET FOR FOREIGN STUDENTS, QUOTED IN *THE NEW YORK TIMES*, APRIL 15, 1985

Whoever wants to know the heart and mind of America had better learn baseball, the rules and realities of the game—and do it by watching first some high-school or small-town teams.

JACQUES BARZUN

Baseball is a red-blooded sport for red-blooded men.
It's no pink tea, and mollycoddles had better stay out.
It's a struggle for supremacy, a survival of the fittest.

TY COBB

———

There are only five things you can do in baseball—
run, throw, catch, hit, and hit with power.

LEO DUROCHER

Pitching is the art of instilling fear.

SANDY KOUFAX

———

The pitcher has got only a ball. I've got a bat. So the percentage in weapons is in my favor and I let the fellow with the ball do the fretting.

HANK AARON

In the beginning I used to make one terrible play a game. Then I got so I'd make one a week and finally I'd pull a bad one about once a month. Now, I'm trying to keep it down to one a season.

Lou Gehrig

Sure I played, did you think I was born at the age of 70 sitting in a dugout trying to manage guys like you?

Casey Stengel, team manager, when asked by Mickey Mantle if he had ever been a ball player

Take a look at them. All nice guys. They'll finish last.
Nice guys finish last.

LEO DUROCHER, OBSERVING THE NEW YORK GIANTS IN 1946

A ball player's got to be kept hungry to become a big
leaguer. That's why no boy from a rich family ever
made the big leagues.

JOE DIMAGGIO

I had a better year than he did.

BABE RUTH, WHEN TOLD THAT PRESIDENT HOOVER MADE LESS THAN THE $80,000 HE WAS DEMANDING IN 1930

I don't know any other ball player who could have done what he did. To be able to hit with everybody yelling at him. He had to block all that out, block out everything but this ball that is coming in at a hundred miles an hour.

PEE WEE REESE, THE CAPTAIN OF THE DODGERS IN THE 1950S, REFERRING TO JACKIE ROBINSON

All the courage and competitiveness of Jackie Robinson affects me to this day. If I patterned my life after anyone it was him, not because he was the first black baseball player in the majors but because he was a hero.

KAREEM ABDUL-JABBAR, *KAREEM* (1990)

A life is not important except in the impact it has on other lives.

JACKIE ROBINSON

Merit will win, it was promised by baseball.

A. BARTLETT GIAMATTI, *TAKE TIME FOR PARADISE* (1989)

The most beautiful thing in the world is a ballpark filled with people.

BILL VEECK, OWNER OF THE CHICAGO WHITE SOX

A professional football team warms up grimly and disparately, like an army on maneuvers: the ground troops here, the tanks there, the artillery and air force over there.

TED SOLOTAROFF, *THE NEW YORK TIMES*, JUNE 11, 1972

American football is an occasion at which dancing girls, bands, tactical huddles and television commercial breaks are interrupted by short bursts of play.

THE TIMES OF LONDON, COMMENTING ON EXHIBITION GAME BETWEEN THE CHICAGO BEARS AND THE DALLAS COWBOYS AT WEMBLEY STADIUM, 1986

Football combines the two worst things about America: it is violence punctuated by committee meetings.

GEORGE F. WILL, POLITICAL COLUMNIST, *INTERNATIONAL HERALD TRIBUNE*, MAY 7, 1990

I am delighted to have you play football. I believe in rough, manly sports.

THEODORE ROOSEVELT, IN A LETTER TO HIS CHILDREN

Gentlemen, it is better to have died as a small boy than to fumble this football.

JOHN HEISMAN

Winning isn't everything, it's the only thing.

VINCE LOMBARDI

Luck is what happens when preparation meets opportunity.

DARRELL ROYAL, QUOTED IN MICHENER, *SPORTS IN AMERICA* (1976)

———•◦•———

I wouldn't ever set out to hurt anyone deliberately unless it was, you know, important—like a league game or something.

DICK BUTKUS, FORMER CHICAGO BEARS LINEBACKER

Football is a game designed to keep coal miners off the streets.

JIMMY BRESLIN

———•••———

I will not permit thirty men to travel four hundred miles to agitate a bag of wind.

ANDREW DICKSON WHITE, CORNELL'S FIRST PRESIDENT (1868–85), REFUSING TO ALLOW THE CORNELL FOOTBALL TEAM TO VISIT MICHIGAN FOR A MATCH

A school without football is in danger of deteriorating into a medieval study hall.

VINCE LOMBARDI

———•———

Baseball developed when we thought nature was a limitless reservoir and we would always live in abundance. Football reflects a different world view; everything has to be fought for, resources are precious, hostile people (guards, monster men) are everywhere and in such a world you have to grab what you can.

ARTHUR ASA BERGER, "FOOTBALL AND TELEVISION," 1976

It's just a bunch of guys with an odd-shaped ball.

BILL PARCELLS

————

Act like you expect to get into the end zone.

JOE PATERNO

I can accept failure. Everyone fails at something. But I can't accept not trying.

MICHAEL JORDAN, *I CAN'T ACCEPT NOT TRYING* (1994)

———

The world chips away at the base of a champion the moment you become one.

KAREEM ABDUL-JABBAR, *KAREEM* (1990)

The athlete approaches the end of his playing days the way old people approach death. But the athlete differs from the old person in that he must continue living. Behind all the years of practice and all the hours of glory waits that inexorable terror of living without the game.

BILL BRADLEY

I can see why fans don't like to watch pro basketball. I don't, either. It's not exciting.

LARRY BIRD

Honey, I forgot to duck.

JACK DEMPSEY, SAID TO HIS WIFE AFTER LOSING A 1926 FIGHT
(RONALD REAGAN USED THE SAME LINE ON NANCY REAGAN AFTER
HE WAS SHOT BY JOHN HINCKLEY.)

Float like a butterfly,
Sting like a bee!
Rumble young man! Rumble!

MUHAMMAD ALI

My business is hurting people.

SUGAR RAY ROBINSON, ADDRESSING THE NEW YORK STATE BOXING
COMMISSION, 1962

I never thought of losing, but now that it's happened,
the only thing is to do it right. That's my obligation
to all the people who believe in me. We all have to
take defeats in life.

MUHAMMAD ALI, STATEMENT AFTER LOSING HIS FIRST FIGHT, TO
KEN NORTON, 1973

Show me a good and gracious loser and I'll show you a loser.

KNUTE ROCKNE, ATTRIBUTED

Vultures! Trash!

JOHN MCENROE, ADDRESSING THE UMPIRE AND THE SPECTATORS AT WIMBLEDON, 1981

In tennis, at the end of the day you're a winner or a loser. You know exactly where you stand.

CHRIS EVERT

———•••———

I strongly believe the black culture spends too much time, energy, and effort raising, praising, and teasing our black children about the dubious glories of professional sports.

ARTHUR ASHE

Experience is a great advantage. The problem is that when you get the experience, you're too damned old to do anything about it.

JIMMY CONNORS

———

I like the moment when I break a man's ego.

BOBBY FISCHER, CHESS PLAYER, 1972

Golf courses are the best place to observe ministers, but none of them are above cheating a bit.

JOHN D. ROCKEFELLER

———

You might as well praise a man for not robbing a bank.

BOBBY JONES, GOLFER, AFTER PENALIZING HIMSELF THE ONE STROKE THAT COST HIM A CHAMPIONSHIP

Then I thought, with the same clubhead speed, the ball's going to go at least six times as far. There's absolutely no drag, so if you do happen to spin it, it won't slice or hook 'cause there's no atmosphere to make it turn.

ASTRONAUT ALAN SHEPARD, TALKING ABOUT HIS FAMOUS DRIVE ON THE LUNAR SURFACE TO *OTTAWA GOLF* MAGAZINE

A lot more people beat me now.

DWIGHT D. EISENHOWER, NOTING A CHANGE IN HIS GOLF GAME AFTER LEAVING THE WHITE HOUSE

The Babe is here. Who's coming in second?

BABE DIDRIKSON ZAHARIAS

Motivation is what gets you started. Habit is what keeps you going.

JIM RYUN

Odd as it sounds, I would rather have the title of cancer survivor than winner of the Tour, because of what it has done for me as a human being, a man, a husband, a son, and a father.

LANCE ARMSTRONG, *IT'S NOT ABOUT THE BIKE* (2000)

The battles that count aren't the ones for gold medals. The struggles within yourself—the invisible, inevitable battles inside all of us—that's where it's at.

JESSE OWENS, SPRINTER, *BLACKTHINK* (1970)

Eleven seconds, you got ten seconds, the countdown going on right now. Five seconds left in the game, do you believe in miracles? YES!

AL MICHAELS, AS THE U.S. ICE HOCKEY TEAM BEAT THE RUSSIANS IN 1980 IN ONE OF THE BIGGEST UPSETS IN OLYMPIC HISTORY

It ain't over till it's over.

YOGI BERRA

We didn't lose the game; we just ran out of time.

VINCE LOMBARDI

There can only be one winner, folks, but isn't that the American way?

HORACE McCOY, *THEY SHOOT HORSES, DON'T THEY?* (1935)

How We Live

What then is the American, this new man?

MICHEL GUILLAUME JEAN DE CREVECOEUR, *LETTERS FROM AN AMERICAN FARMER*, 1782

The overwhelming majority of Americans are possessed of two great qualities—a sense of humor and a sense of proportion.

FRANKLIN D. ROOSEVELT, QUOTED IN *THE WIT AND WISDOM OF FRANKLIN D. ROOSEVELT* (1982)

In Europe life is histrionic and dramatized, and in America, except when it is trying to be European, it is direct and sincere.

WILLIAM DEAN HOWELLS, U.S. NOVELIST, *HARPER'S*, 1899

Behold, I do not give lectures or a little charity, When I give I give myself.

WALT WHITMAN, *SONG OF MYSELF*, 1855

Intrepid, unprincipled, reckless, predatory, with boundless ambition, civilized in externals but a savage at heart, America is, or may yet be, the Paul Jones of nations.

HERMAN MELVILLE, 1855

I found there a country with thirty-two religions and only one sauce.

CHARLES MAURICE DE TALLEYRAND-PÉRIGORD (1754–1838)

America is the only nation in history which miraculously has gone directly from barbarism to degeneration without the usual interval of civilization.

GEORGES CLEMENCEAU, FRENCH STATESMAN (1841–1929)

It is veneer, rouge, aestheticism, art museums, new theaters, etc. that make America impotent. The good things are football, kindness, and jazz bands.

GEORGE SANTAYANA, AMERICAN PHILOSOPHER, LETTER, 1927

In every American there is an air of incorrigible innocence, which seems to conceal a diabolical cunning.

A. E. HOUSMAN, BRITISH POET (1859–1936)

In a land which is fully settled, most men must accept their local environment or try to change it by political means. In America, on the other hand, to move on and make a fresh start somewhere else is still the normal reaction to dissatisfaction and failure.

W. H. AUDEN, INTRODUCTION TO *THE FABER BOOK OF MODERN AMERICAN VERSE* (1956)

I went to the woods because I wished to live deliberately, to front only the essential facts of life, and see if I could not learn what it had to teach, and not, when I came to die, discover that I had not lived.

HENRY DAVID THOREAU, "WHERE I LIVED, AND WHAT I LIVED FOR," *WALDEN* (1854)

The history of this country was made largely by people who wanted to be left alone. Those who could not
thrive when left to themselves never felt at ease in
America.

ERIC HOFFER, *REFLECTIONS ON THE HUMAN CONDITION* (1973)

I think if you'd like to renew your acquaintance with yourself, you could do worse than spend time on a deer stand. Sometimes the hours go quickly, and you become part of the scene. Sometimes each half-minute is torture.

DAVID MAMET, "DEER HUNTING," MEN'S JOURNAL, 1914

———

Our ancestors were laborers, not lawyers.

THOMAS JEFFERSON, "A SUMMARY VIEW OF THE RIGHTS OF BRITISH AMERICANS," 1774

One can not be an American by going about saying that one is an American. It is necessary to feel America, like America, love America and then work.

Georgia O'Keeffe, 1926

Character, not circumstances, makes the man.

Booker T. Washington, 1896

You might as well fall flat on your face as lean over too far backward.

JAMES THURBER, 1939

———•••———

Whenever you are asked if you can do a job, tell 'em, "Certainly, I can!" Then get busy and find out how to do it.

THEODORE ROOSEVELT

What the country needs is dirtier fingernails and cleaner minds.

WILL ROGERS

In America few people will trust you unless you are irreverent.

NORMAN MAILER, PREFACE TO *THE PRESIDENTIAL PAPERS* (1963)

I never met a man I didn't like.

WILL ROGERS, EPITAPH

The report of my death has been greatly exaggerated.

MARK TWAIN'S RESPONSE TO A NEWSPAPER REPORTER INVESTIGATING THE RUMOR THAT HE HAD DIED, 1896

Except in a few well-publicized instances, the rigorous practice of rugged individualism usually leads to poverty, ostracism and disgrace.

LEWIS H. LAPHAM, *MONEY AND CLASS IN AMERICA* (1988)

High school is closer to the core of the American experience than anything else I can think of.

KURT VONNEGUT, INTRODUCTION, *OUR TIMES IS NOW* (1970)

Americans are like a rich father who wishes he knew how to give his son the hardships that made him rich.

ROBERT FROST

No culture on earth outside of mid-century suburban America has ever deployed one woman per child without simultaneously assigning her such major productive activities as weaving, farming, gathering, temple maintenance, and tent-building.

BARBARA EHRENREICH, "STOP IRONING THE DIAPERS," *THE WORST YEARS OF OUR LIVES* (1989)

I love to see a young girl go out and grab the world by the lapels. Life's a bitch. You've got to go out and kick ass.

MAYA ANGELOU, INTERVIEW, 1986

Some of us were ambivalent, but we don't do ambivalence well in America. We do courage of our convictions. We do might makes right. Ambivalence is French.

ANNA QUINDLEN, *THINKING OUT LOUD* (1993)

Courage is the price that Life exacts for granting peace.

AMELIA EARHART, THE FIRST WOMAN TO FLY SOLO OVER BOTH THE ATLANTIC AND PACIFIC OCEANS, 1927

America is the most grandiose experiment the world has seen, but, I am afraid, it is not going to be a success.

SIGMUND FREUD (1856–1939)

Sex. In America an obsession. In other parts of the world a fact.

MARLENE DIETRICH, GERMAN-BORN U.S. ACTRESS, 1962

They think that Miss America belongs to them! That they can touch her and give her a kiss on the cheek— or even on the lips!

ELLIE ROSS, TRAVELING COMPANION FOR MISS AMERICAS. AS QUOTED IN *MISS AMERICA* (1991)

If there is any country on earth where the course of true love may be expected to run smooth, it is America.

HARRIET MARTINEAU, BRITISH WRITER, "MARRIAGE," *SOCIETY IN AMERICA*, VOL. III (1837)

The unreal is natural, so natural that it makes of unreality the most natural of anything natural. That is what America does, and that is what America is.

GERTRUDE STEIN, "I CAME AND HERE I AM" (1936)

Nothing is real unless it happens on television.

DANIEL J. BOORSTIN, 1978

———

In modern America, anyone who attempts to write satirically about the events of the day finds it difficult to concoct a situation so bizarre that it may not actually come to pass while his article is still on the presses.

CALVIN TRILLIN, 1982

In America nothing dies easier than tradition.

RUSSELL BAKER, 1991

Myths and legends die hard in America. We love them for the extra dimension they provide, the illusion of near-infinite possibility. Weird heroes and mold-breaking champions exist as living proof to those who need it that the tyranny of "the rat race" is not yet final.

HUNTER S. THOMPSON, "THOSE DARING YOUNG MEN IN THEIR FLYING MACHINES . . . AIN'T WHAT THEY USED TO BE!," 1969

Where we come from in America no longer signi-
fies—it's where we go, and what we do when we get
there, that tells us who we are.

ANNA QUINDLEN, *THINKING OUT LOUD* (1993)

⸻

Races didn't bother the Americans. They were some-
thing a lot better than any race. They were a People.
They were the first self-constituted, self-created
People in the history of the world.

ARCHIBALD MACLEISH, "THE AMERICAN CAUSE," 1940

People, when they first come to America, whether as travelers or settlers, become aware of a new and agreeable feeling: that the whole country is their oyster.

ALISTAIR COOKE, *AMERICA* (1973)

There is a New America every morning when we wake up. It is upon us whether we will it or not.

ADLAI E. STEVENSON

It is a fabulous country, the only fabulous country; it is the only place where miracles not only happen, but where they happen all the time.

THOMAS WOLFE

America is a vast conspiracy to make you happy.

JOHN UPDIKE, 1980

Index